A GUIDEBOOK OF
Promising Practices

Facilitating College Students'
SPIRITUAL DEVELOPMENT

A GUIDEBOOK OF
Promising Practices

Facilitating College Students'
SPIRITUAL DEVELOPMENT

Jennifer A. Lindholm • Melissa L. Millora
Leslie M. Schwartz • Hanna Song Spinosa

ISBN-13: 978-1456456856
ISBN-10: 1456456857
BISAC: Education / Students & Student Life

Printed in the United States of America
FIRST EDITION

FOREWORD

The idea for this guidebook grew out of a national study of students' spiritual development, which was initiated at UCLA's Higher Education Research Institute in 2003 under a grant from the John Templeton Foundation. The major findings from that study, which are reported in the recently released book, *Cultivating the Spirit: How College Can Enhance Students' Inner Lives* (authored by the two of us and our colleague Jennifer Lindholm), convinced us that it was time for higher education to increase its efforts to promote students' spiritual development. We believe that assisting more students to grow spiritually will help to create a new generation of young adults who are more caring, more globally aware, and more committed to social justice than previous generations. At the same time, it will enable them to respond with greater equanimity to the many stresses and tensions of our rapidly changing technological society.

This conclusion was supported by a number of our study's specific findings: that a large majority of contemporary students are actively engaged in a spiritual quest; that many expect their colleges to assist them in this quest; and that our colleges and universities have demonstrated the capacity to facilitate students' spiritual development in many of their curricular and co-curricular programs. Our study also shows that providing students with more opportunities to touch base with their "inner selves" will facilitate growth in their academic and leadership skills, contribute to their intellectual self-confidence and psychological well-being, and enhance their satisfaction with the college experience.

If a college or university wishes to undertake new initiatives that will foster students' spiritual growth, it is useful to know something about what other institutions are doing. We decided to produce this guidebook in order to provide faculty and staff with a broad sampling of current programs and practices that are designed to encourage students to explore their inner lives and to facilitate students' spiritual development.

In this search to learn from the field, we have been impressed with the energy, creativity, and commitment already being shown by many higher education colleagues who have created courses, co-curricular programs, and other strategies to assist students in their spiritual journeys.

More than 400 institutions responded to our call for examples of promising practices. What they have reported back to us ranges from undergraduate degree programs, majors, and minors to specialized courses and seminars dealing with many of the "big questions," which touch on issues of morality, love, suffering, social justice, and social transformation. They incorporate practices ranging from meditation and yoga to stress management. They involve diverse subjects such as interfaith relations or depression, as well as practical issues such as mindful living in residence halls and the development of life skills. Some institutions have established centers devoted to activities that facilitate spiritual development; others have created physical spaces for meditation or reflection. A number of institutions also provide opportunities for the spiritual development of faculty and staff, assisting personnel who may wish to undertake this important work.

Major responsibility for producing this guidebook has been assumed by our *Cultivating the Spirit* coauthor, Jennifer Lindholm, together with three current and former members of our project team: Melissa ("Lisa") Millora, Leslie Schwartz, and Hanna Spinosa.[1] These colleagues have done a superb job in canvassing colleges and universities across the country to determine promising practices that are already in place, and especially in organizing the considerable amount of information that they received in user-friendly fashion. We all owe a debt of gratitude to them and the hundreds of people on campuses who provided us with information about their programs.

We were pleased to learn that so many institutions of virtually every type are already involved in a wide variety of innovative programs and practices to enhance and enrich the inner lives of their students. It is our hope that the publication of this guidebook will encourage many other colleges and universities to undertake similar efforts.

Helen S. Astin
Alexander W. Astin
Co-Principal Investigators

---

[1] The authors of the guidebook are listed alphabetically.

PREFACE

Throughout the course of the *Spirituality in Higher Education* project, higher education professionals have expressed to our research team their desire to learn how to facilitate students' spiritual development via campus initiatives. They ask: "As a professor, for example, how might I create a course that explores spirituality within the context of my particular subject matter?"; "as a student leader, how can I work with my peers to bring awareness and attention to the different ways in which people experience spirituality in order to promote cross-cultural understanding?"; or, "as an administrator, what would be an effective approach for engaging different segments of the campus community in developing a strategic plan focused on students' spiritual development?"

In response, we have conceptualized *Promising Practices* as a resource for those within higher education who are interested in attending to issues of spirituality, meaning, and purpose as part of the undergraduate experience. This guidebook includes descriptions of some of the practices, programs, and syllabi that campus personnel have shared with us. We hope that these descriptions serve as models and spark new ideas for promoting spiritual development on campus.

CONTENT AND ORGANIZATION OF THIS GUIDEBOOK

Part I, "Spirituality in Higher Education," describes briefly the background of the research project and explains how the research team conceptualized spirituality.

Part II, "Spirituality on Campus Today," offers an overview of contemporary trends, discusses spirituality in the context of today's students and campuses, and provides examples of how various campus groups (administrators, faculty and academic affairs personnel, student affairs professionals, and student leaders) can engage students in spiritual development work.

Part III, "Promising Practices," highlights some of the specific practices and programs that colleagues from across the country have shared with us. These resources are grouped into the following main headings: Curricular

Initiatives and Teaching Strategies, Co-Curricular Programs and Services, and Campus-wide Efforts. While you may anticipate that one of these categories is most directly relevant to your particular role on campus, we encourage you to explore each section. For additional details about selected programs and practices contained within this guidebook, we encourage you to contact colleagues at those institutions (see Contributors, p. 101).

ACKNOWLEDGMENTS

Numerous individuals and groups have contributed to this guidebook. We thank the John Templeton Foundation for its generous support, which made this work possible, as well as the research our team conducted through the *Spirituality in Higher Education* project. We are also grateful to all those who responded to our requests for information about their campuses' innovative practices. (A list of those individuals can be found at the back of this book.) We also thank the UCLA Graduate School of Education & Information Studies and the Higher Education Research Institute for their support of the *Spirituality in Higher Education* project over the last decade. Finally, we are tremendously appreciative of the roles that Helen ("Lena") Astin and Alexander ("Sandy") Astin have played in our lives as teachers, mentors, colleagues, and friends.

CONTENTS

PART I
SPIRITUALITY IN HIGHER EDUCATION

PART I

SPIRITUALITY IN HIGHER EDUCATION

PROJECT BACKGROUND

In early 2003, a UCLA research team led by Alexander Astin, Helen Astin, and Jennifer Lindholm embarked on a seven-year journey to examine how students' spiritual qualities change during their undergraduate years, and what role the college experience plays in facilitating their spiritual development. Titled *Spirituality in Higher Education: A National Study of College Students' Search for Meaning and Purpose*, the project was funded by the John Templeton Foundation. It was the first national longitudinal study of college students' spiritual growth and also focused on how college and university faculty view the intersections between spirituality and higher education.

The primary reason for undertaking the study was a shared belief among the lead researchers that spirituality is fundamental to students' lives. The "big" questions" that preoccupy students are essentially spiritual questions: Who am I? What is my purpose? What is the meaning of life? What kind of person do I want to become? What sort of world do I want to help to create? When we speak of students' "spiritual quest," we are essentially speaking of their efforts to seek answers to such questions.

How students deal with these questions has important implications for many practical decisions they will have to make, including their choices of courses, majors, and careers, not to mention whether they opt to stay in college or drop out and whether they decide to pursue postgraduate study. Seeking answers to these questions is also directly relevant to the development of personal qualities, such as self-understanding, empathy, caring, and social responsibility.

Another compelling motivation for engaging in this work was a collective sentiment of the researchers that, over time, the relative amount of atten-

3

tion that colleges and universities devote to the "inner" and "outer" aspects of students' lives has become significantly imbalanced. That sentiment, along with growing unease about our institutions and our society, has led some of us to start talking much more openly about the importance of cultivating "inner," or spiritual, qualities.

Envisioning campus communities in which the life of the mind and the life of the spirit are mutually celebrated, supported, and sustained necessitates that our higher education community must reconsider our traditional ways of being and doing. We must be open to broadening our existing frames of reference and willing to look closely not just at what we do (or do not do) on a daily basis, but *why*, considering the motivations behind our thoughts, beliefs, and actions.

To support those efforts, we developed *Promising Practices*, a guidebook for those within higher education who are interested in incorporating elements of spirituality, meaning, and purpose into campus life. In this guidebook, we highlight both campus-wide initiatives and specifically tailored institutional practices, aiming to supplement existing programs and courses with teaching methods and practices that facilitate spiritual development. We envision that others can potentially adapt these practices to support their own institutional interests and needs. As educators, researchers, practitioners, and students who are committed to supporting students' spiritual development, we are hopeful that work to facilitate students' spiritual development may continue to expand and flourish.

CONCEPTUALIZING SPIRITUALITY

From the project's outset, the *Spirituality in Higher Education* research team has conceptualized spirituality as pointing to our inner, subjective life, as contrasted to the objective domain of observable behavior and material objects. Spirituality involves our affective experiences at least as much as it does our reasoning and logic. It is reflected in the values and ideals that we hold most dear, our sense of who we are and where we come from, our beliefs about why we are here—the meaning and purpose we see in our lives—and our connectedness to each other and to the world around us. Spirituality also captures those aspects of our experience that are not easy to define or talk about, such as intuition, inspiration, the mysterious, and the mystical.

We acknowledge that each individual will view his or her spirituality in a unique way. For some, traditional religious beliefs compose the core of their spirituality; for others, such beliefs or traditions may play little or no part. For those of us who conducted the *Spirituality in Higher Education* study, the focal point of the research project was to discern the level and intensity of spiritual experience among college students and to understand how colleges can support students in their growth through this experience; it was not to determine how students define their spirituality or what particular meaning they make of their lives.

Framed by five of the measures created during the longitudinal study, members of the research team developed the following definition:

> Spirituality is a multifaceted quality that involves an active quest for answers to life's "big questions" (Spiritual Quest), a global worldview that transcends ethnocentrism and egocentrism (Ecumenical Worldview), a sense of caring and compassion for others (Ethic of Caring) coupled with a lifestyle that includes service to others (Charitable Involvement), and a capacity to maintain one's sense of calm and centeredness, especially in times of stress (Equanimity).

In the next section, we define and describe each of these measures in greater depth.

SPIRITUALITY MEASURES

One of the goals in conducting the *Spirituality in Higher Education* study was to develop measures that address various dimensions of spirituality and religiousness. Toward that end, the team searched for clusters of survey-questionnaire items that formed coherent patterns reflective of underlying traits. Through this process, we identified five spiritual measures: Spiritual Quest, Equanimity, Ethic of Caring, Charitable Involvement, and Ecumenical Worldview.

SPIRITUAL QUEST

Spiritual Quest is at the heart of students' spiritual development. It captures the degree to which an individual is actively searching for meaning and purpose, desiring to find wisdom, and seeking answers to life's mysteries and "big questions." Each of the individual items that compose this heavily process-oriented measure includes words such as "finding," "attaining," "seeking," "developing," "searching," or "becoming."

EQUANIMITY

Equanimity may well be the prototypic quality of a spiritual person. It measures the extent to which the student is able to find meaning in times of hardship, feels at peace or centered, sees each day as a gift, and feels good about the direction of his or her life. Equanimity plays an important role in the quality of undergraduate students' lives because it helps shape how they respond to their experiences, particularly those that are potentially stressful.

ETHIC OF CARING

Ethic of Caring reflects our sense of caring and concern about the welfare of others and the world around us. These feelings are expressed in wanting to help those who are troubled and to alleviate suffering. It includes a concern about social justice issues and an interest in the welfare of one's community and the environment, as well as a commitment to political activism.

CHARITABLE INVOLVEMENT

In contrast to Ethic of Caring, which emphasizes "caring about," *Charitable Involvement* emphasizes "caring for." This behavioral measure includes activities such as participating in community service, donating money to charity, and helping friends with personal problems.

ECUMENICAL WORLDVIEW

Ecumenical Worldview reflects a global worldview that transcends ethnocentrism and egocentrism. It indicates the extent to which the student is interested in different religious traditions, seeks to understand other countries and cultures, feels a strong connection to all humanity, believes in the goodness of all people, accepts others as they are, and believes that all life is interconnected and that love is at the root of all the great religions.

These five spiritual measures, which help to articulate various aspects of individuals' experiences, are critical aspects of college student development. By researching how these measures interface with students' college experience, the *Spirituality in Higher Education* research team has gained a deeper understanding of the impact that higher education has on students' spiritual development. Selected study findings are discussed in the next section along with implications for supporting and fostering students' spiritual growth in college.

PRACTICE INFORMED BY RESEARCH

The 2004-07 longitudinal College Students' Beliefs and Values (CSBV) Survey entailed analysis of extensive data collected from 14,527 students attending 136 colleges and universities nationwide. To support that work, the research team conducted individual and focus-group interviews with students, and surveyed and interviewed faculty.[2] The findings provide a powerful argument in support of the proposition that higher education should attend more purposefully to students' spiritual development.

In the book *Cultivating the Spirit: How College Can Enhance Students' Inner Lives* (Astin, Astin, & Lindholm, 2011), the *Spirituality in Higher Education* project's lead researchers detail how students change during college on each of the five spiritual measures described earlier: **Spiritual Quest, Equanimity, Ethic of Caring, Charitable Involvement,** and **Ecumenical Worldview.** Changes over time on five religious measures—**Religious Commitment, Religious Engagement, Religious/Social Conservatism, Religious Skepticism,** and **Religious Struggle**—are also examined. Ultimately considered are how student change on each measure affects traditional undergraduate education outcomes (e.g. academic skills, satisfaction with college), and how different college experiences tend to impact students' spiritual development.

---

[2] Survey questionnaires and interview protocols are available on the project website: www.spirituality.ucla.edu.

Findings from the longitudinal study show that when they enter college as freshmen:

- Students have very high levels of spiritual interest and involvement. Many are actively engaged in a spiritual quest and are exploring meaning and purpose in life. They also display high levels of religious commitment and involvement.

- Students also have high expectations for the role their educational institutions will play in their emotional and spiritual development. They place great value on their colleges enhancing their self-understanding, helping them develop personal values, and encouraging their expression of spirituality.

Additionally, during college:

- **Religious Engagement** declines somewhat, yet students' spiritual qualities grow substantially.

- Students show the greatest degree of growth in the five spiritual qualities if they are actively engaged in "inner work" through self-reflection, contemplation, and/or meditation.

- Students also show substantial increases in **Spiritual Quest** when their faculty encourage them to explore questions of meaning and purpose or otherwise show support for their spiritual development.

- Engagement in most forms of **Charitable Involvement**—community service work, helping friends with personal problems, donating money to charity—promotes the development of other spiritual qualities.

- Growth in **Equanimity** enhances students' grade-point average, leadership skills, psychological well-being, self-rated ability to get along with other races and cultures, and satisfaction with college.

- Growth in **Ethic of Caring** and **Ecumenical Worldview** enhances students' interest in postgraduate study, self-rated ability to get along with other races and cultures, and commitment to promoting racial understanding.

- Educational experiences and practices that promote spiritual development—especially service learning, interdisciplinary courses, study abroad, self-reflection, and meditation—have uniformly positive effects on traditional college outcomes.

- Providing students with more opportunities to connect with their "inner selves" facilitates growth in students' academic and leadership skills, contributes to their intellectual self-confidence and psychological well-being, and enhances their satisfaction with college.

These findings paint a picture of how specific college experiences can influence the spiritual growth and development of traditionally aged students during the undergraduate years. For those interested in more detail about the development and utilization of these measures in our research, please see the project website (www.spirituality.ucla.edu) or *Cultivating the Spirit*. In Part II, we discuss the current context of spirituality on campus, and general strategies for integrating spirituality into higher education.

PART II
SPIRITUALITY ON CAMPUS TODAY

PART II
SPIRITUALITY ON CAMPUS TODAY

As detailed in *Cultivating the Spirit*, America's higher education system currently is being challenged to focus more purposely on students' holistic development, including nurturing the spiritual identities of students, faculty, and staff. Holistic student learning and development include "vocational, professional, intellectual, cognitive, social, civic, political, moral, ethical, spiritual, and religious dimensions, and focus on values clarification and character development" (Trautvetter, 2007, pp. 238-239).

While the philosophy that colleges and universities should educate the whole student—mind, body, and spirit—is not new, institutions' approaches to this work have varied over the more than 300 years since the first American college was established. At many of the earliest colleges, attention to the *spirit* once took the form of character development through training in moral philosophy and ethics. Over time, however, this focus has waned (Cohen, 1998; Reuben, 1996).

Today, particularly in secular institutions, many campus personnel tend to conceptualize spirituality as linked inextricably with religion. By extension, they believe that apart from the work of their religious life colleagues, attending to spiritual aspects of students' lives has no legitimate place within the academy. As elaborated in *Cultivating the Spirit,* however, secular institutions can provide a rich environment for students to explore the spiritual dimension of their lives. Indeed, the broad formative roles that colleges and universities of all types continue to play in our society, combined with their long-standing commitment to liberal learning, position them to attend to the development of both mind and spirit.

SUPPORTING STUDENTS' SPIRITUAL DEVELOPMENT

When they enter college as new freshmen, many students express high expectations for their own spiritual development. More than eight in 10, for example, report that "to find my purpose in life" is at least a "somewhat" important reason for attending college. Fully half say it's a "very important" reason. Two-thirds of new freshmen also say that it is either "very important" or "essential" that college "helps you develop your personal values" and "enhances your self-understanding" (Astin, Astin, & Lindholm, 2011). Findings from the *Spirituality in Higher Education* project support the notion that many students come to college today seeking spaces where their contributions and self-worth matter beyond salaries, GPAs, or the prestige of future careers (see e.g. Howe & Strauss, 2007).

The undergraduate experience offers students numerous opportunities to explore issues of meaning, purpose, and faith as they engage with peers, faculty, and staff who embody various backgrounds, beliefs, and practices. Exposure to new and diverse perspectives is valuable in challenging students to compare, examine, and clarify their own personal beliefs and values in a communal setting (see e.g. Palmer, 1990). Our project findings, as detailed in *Cultivating the Spirit*, support the notion that exposure to diverse people, cultures, and ideas—through study abroad, interdisciplinary coursework, leadership education, service learning, and other forms of civic engagement—helps students better understand, and value, multiple perspectives. These capacities are especially critical given the complex social, economic, and political challenges of our time.

As students encounter difference in college, they are challenged to grow and change. For many, college may be the first time they have questioned "truth" and "reality." Indeed, the college experience can be critical in helping students explore and clarify their faith, beliefs, and values. Experiencing "disequilibrium" or spiritual struggle provides students with opportunities to analyze their life circumstances and the deeper meaning and purpose that they are seeking as they strive to live more connected, integrated lives (Fowler, 1981; Parks, 2000). The challenge for campus personnel, then, becomes how to effectively address issues related to the spiritual dimension of students' lives.

THE ROLE OF CAMPUS PERSONNEL IN FACILITATING STUDENTS' SPIRITUAL DEVELOPMENT

Findings from the *Spirituality in Higher Education* longitudinal study and those reported in *Cultivating the Spirit* indicate that many students are eager to explore their own spiritual identities and come to a deeper understanding of meaning, purpose, and faith in their lives. These findings echo the call of other scholars to: 1) amplify the importance they place on spiritual growth, authenticity, purpose, and meaning and 2) view spiritual issues and considerations as legitimate concerns within our campus communities (Braskamp, Trautvetter, & Ward, 2006; Chickering, Dalton, & Stamm, 2006).

Within each campus, there are multiple ways for campus personnel to support students' spiritual development. Appreciating that many effective institutional practices are the products of collaborative efforts, below we provide suggestions for how individual members of a campus community can promote students' spiritual development.

ADMINISTRATORS

We consider administrators to be members of the campus whose student interactions are more functional in nature. Campus administrators may be admissions officers, financial aid counselors, directors of campus ministry, deans of religious life, deans of students, vice presidents, provosts, and senior campus executives. Within these positions, administrators can both directly and indirectly support students' spiritual development by:

- Considering how mission and vision statements, along with strategic plans, can communicate an institution's commitment or openness to supporting students' spiritual development;

- Fostering a campus climate that supports open conversations about spiritual development by modeling these dialogues with colleagues and students;

- Creating and designating physical spaces for reflective practice; and

- Developing organizational structures to coordinate, implement, and maintain practices and programs that encourage spiritual development and facilitate campus-wide collaboration.

FACULTY AND ACADEMIC PERSONNEL

The realm of Academic Affairs refers to faculty members along with lecturers, teaching assistants, researchers, and other academic members of the campus community. The amount of time that faculty and other academic personnel spend on research, teaching, and service varies by campus, but faculty may find ways to incorporate spiritual development work into any of their areas of responsibility. Strategies include:

- Encouraging spiritually related discussions within the classroom (e.g. including course content about the "Big Questions" or spiritual practices);

- Exposing students to various values, belief systems, and ways of living to build respect for differences across various disciplinary settings;

- Sharing personal experiences of spiritual struggle or quest for meaning, purpose, and truth with colleagues and students when appropriate;

- Providing emotional support for students in crisis and making appropriate referrals to student affairs professionals;

- Recognizing that students have lives beyond the walls of the classroom and exercising compassion where these issues come into play; and

- Challenging students to search for ways to find meaning and purpose within their field of study and related career choices.

STUDENT AFFAIRS PROFESSIONALS

For the purposes of this guidebook, we consider student affairs professional to be practitioners whose primary roles involve educating, supporting, and challenging students outside the classroom. These practitioners often work in academic advising, career services, health and wellness centers, residential life, diversity and multicultural education, campus recreation, cultural centers, and student activities and leadership offices. Student affairs professionals can help facilitate students' spiritual development by:

- Learning more about spiritual development and the role it plays in students' lives;

- Encouraging students to take time away from their busy lives to reflect on their experiences in light of their beliefs and values;

- Incorporating reflective practices into the meetings or leadership trainings of student organizations;

- Developing more experiential education initiatives to help students make connections between their lives, the world around them, and what they are learning in the classroom;

- Exposing students to different values, belief systems, and different ways of living to build respect for differences within various environments;

- Offering opportunities for students to engage in health and recreation practices that promote peace and inner harmony to model balance for students;

- Helping students cultivate an ethic of caring and learn ways to promote community welfare;

- Developing and coordinating educational programming to promote wholeness and holistic education; and

- Supporting students in crisis by making appropriate referrals.

STUDENT LEADERS

Many students are engaged in leadership activities and hold positions of influence on campus. Other student leaders may not have a title or position, but they are willing to make an impact on campus. Student leaders have a unique kind of credibility with peers and can reach other students in ways that staff, faculty, administrators, and parents cannot. Student leaders can help foster a spiritual campus climate by:

- Taking time to consider personal beliefs and values and how they connect to the decisions made and experiences pursued during college;

- Modeling contemplative practice, balance, and self-management, while encouraging other student leaders and peers to do the same;

- Incorporating reflective practices into regular meetings or leadership trainings;

- Giving input to instructors and staff about how they can help facilitate students' spiritual development;

- Gathering information about students' interest in programs that can foster spiritual development, and communicating the results to campus decision-makers; and

- Developing and coordinating programming to foster spiritual development and involving other students and campus stakeholders in the planning processes.

The ideas in this section offer merely a snapshot of the ways in which members of the campus community can support the spiritual dimension of students' lives. In Part III, we supplement the general ideas offered here with specific examples of current curricular and co-curricular practices to facilitate students' spiritual development, along with related campus-wide initiatives and faculty/ staff development efforts. Professional groups and organizations, including the Association for the Contemplative Mind in Higher Education, and the NASPA Knowledge Community on Spirituality, among others, also provide critical networks for those engaged in this work.

PART III
PROMISING
PRACTICES

PART III:
PROMISING PRACTICES

Since the very beginning of the *Spirituality in Higher Education* project, higher education practitioners have approached us with enthusiasm about this research and its applications on campuses. In response, our initial effort to collect information about existing campus practices in spring 2005 centered around collecting syllabi from courses in which faculty incorporated assignments and other activities to facilitate undergraduate students' spiritual inquiry and awareness.[1] In 2006, our UCLA-based research team hosted a National Institute on Spirituality in Higher Education which brought together teams from 10 diverse campuses to discuss possibilities for integrating spirituality into the curriculum and co-curriculum. Later, after a call put forth by our research team in 2007, faculty and administrators from 40 campuses across the country sent us information on their campus' curricular and co-curricular practices designed to support the spiritual development of undergraduate students.

In summer 2010, we expanded the pool of information by surveying vice presidents for student affairs, vice presidents for academic affairs, and campus ministry directors or chaplains at 1,580 four-year colleges nationwide. The intent of e-mailing the questionnaire to three specific officials at each institution was to capture the range of perspectives held by different campus groups. The online questionnaire covered a variety of topics from specific practices and programs that promote student spiritual development to faculty spiritual development.[2]

---

[1] Syllabi are available at http://spirituality.ucla.edu/publications/newsletters/2/syllabi.php

[2] For a copy of the survey questionnaire, please see Appendix A.

PARTICIPATING INSTITUTIONS

We were pleased to receive a very diverse sample of responses to our requests for sharing promising practices that support students' spiritual development. The following is a list of the responding institutions that are members of various higher education associations. Ultimately, we received 570 responses from 407 institutions.

Total Number of Participating Campuses[3] 435

Association of American Universities...22

Public Institutions
American Association of State Colleges and Universities 47
Association of Public Land Grant Universities..................................35

Private Institutions
Annapolis Group 59

Other Private Religious Colleges
Association of Catholic Colleges and Universities 83
Council for Christian Colleges and Universities...............................48
International Association of Methodist-Related Schools,
     Colleges, and Universities...45
Association of Presbyterian Colleges and Universities......................21
Lutheran Colleges and Universities...11

PRACTICES HIGHLIGHTED IN THIS GUIDEBOOK

This guidebook is not intended to be a complete directory of all existing practices that promote students' spiritual development. Due to space limitations, we could not include descriptions of all the practices that we received.

---

[3] For six campuses included in this count, Promising Practices information was obtained from campus websites rather than provided directly by campus personnel via survey responses or other submissions.

Instead, we have sought to provide readers with a broad survey of practices from a diversity of institutions.

Our goal is to promote information-sharing and spark discussion for all who are interested in the spiritual development of college students. Whether you desire to implement a campus-wide initiative or provide resources for students who want to start an organization centered on spiritual issues, this guidebook can serve as a starting point for identifying other campuses where similar and successful initiatives have been implemented. The practices that follow are divided into curricular, co-curricular, and campus-wide efforts.

CURRICULAR INITIATIVES AND TEACHING STRATEGIES

This section highlights examples of the many ways that an institution's curricular initiatives may facilitate students' spiritual development. Examples include: *Academic Degree Programs, Courses and Curricular Innovations, and Teaching Methods.*

ACADEMIC DEGREE PROGRAMS

At many campuses, students can pursue courses of study that encourage exploration of spirituality or religion. One venue is through traditional baccalaureate degree-granting programs housed in religious studies departments. Another possibility is to offer specially-designed concentrations or interdisciplinary majors and minors. Below are some examples:

- At **Boston College**, elective academic programs that explore spirituality and religion include a **Faith, Peace, and Justice minor, Jewish Studies minor, and Islamic and Middle Eastern Studies minor.** Core philosophy courses explore ultimate questions of meaning and purpose. Some students fulfill these core requirements through the PULSE program, which links theology and philosophy coursework to 10 hours of community service per week.

- **University of Michigan** offers a **Program in Creativity and Consciousness,** funded by the Office of the Provost with support from the School of Music,

Theatre, and Dance. The traditional course load is supplemented by opportunities to participate in: a monthly gathering to explore improvisation across a wide variety of disciplines; a think-tank called the "deep inquiry group" that focuses on big questions of consciousness, human development, and current events; faculty study groups that explore issues of creativity and consciousness inter-disciplinarily; and lecture series that invite a wide range of speakers. Currently, the program offers a **B.A. of Fine Arts in Jazz and Contemplative Studies.**

Other academic programs:

- **Brown University:** Scholarly Concentration in Contemplative Studies, a branch of the Contemplative Studies Initiative

- **George Fox University:** Peace and Justice minor

- **George Mason University:** 16-credit academic minor that includes courses in mindfulness, consciousness, and meaning, based in the Center for Consciousness and Transformation

COURSES AND OTHER CURRICULAR INNOVATIONS THAT PROMOTE SPIRITUAL QUALITIES

Faculty across the country from a variety of disciplines have developed a multitude of courses to incorporate spirituality into the curriculum. Topics that are related to spirituality and lend themselves to this strategy include death and dying, ethics, the meaning of life, stress and health, values, and moral philosophy, among others. Faculty from around the country also shared with the team 39 sample syllabi, which are available online at http://spirituality.ucla.edu/publications/newsletters/2/syllabi.php.

Instructors responsible for the professional preparation of teachers, counselors, or business leaders have opportunities to engage students in curricular activities that will help prepare them to incorporate spiritual practices into their future work. Below are selected examples of courses, and other curricular ideas that have been shared with us, which are categorized here by their focus on "big questions" (spiritual exploration), spirituality and wellness, or religious studies courses.

Courses Focused on the "Big Questions" or Spiritual Exploration
Faculty are well positioned to challenge students to think about the "big questions" such as: *Who am I? Why am I here? What is my purpose in life?* Examples of these types of courses include the following:

- **Carnegie Mellon** developed a "Big Questions Initiative" with the goal of engaging faculty and students in conversations about personal values, morals, and responsibility. Eventual plans involve expanding the program into the entire first-year residence hall system.

- **Franklin W. Olin College of Engineering** offers the "What Is I?" course that encourages students to explore their psychological development, personalities, purpose in life, and so forth. This course is one of several Arts, Humanities, and Social Sciences courses in a curriculum otherwise entirely devoted to engineering.

- **Salem College** has a **Signature Program** that is designed to lead students along a path of self-knowledge, community service and career preparation. Each student is required to take courses within the program that address service learning, global perspective, cross-cultural awareness, and the "big questions."

- **Stanford University** offers a class called **The Meaning of Life: Moral and Spiritual Inquiry Through Literature**, which combines traditional classroom work, field trips, weekend activities, and a living-learning experience in an intense three-week course. Stanford also offers a class called **Spirituality and Nonviolent Urban and Social Transformation**, based on the notion that a life of engagement in social transformation is often built on a foundation of spiritual and religious commitments. The class incorporates film, texts, and service, and utilizes case studies of nonviolent social change agents to examine the theory and principles of nonviolence as well as religious and spiritual issues.

- *The Semester Within* at the **University of Redlands** is a documentary film about students' curricular experiences in which they talk about the challenges and benefits of interior learning and meditation. Students study moral exemplars such as Mother Teresa, the Dalai Lama, Gandhi, and Nelson Mandela. They are also encouraged to use meditation techniques in their service learning endeavors.

Other campuses with similar courses:

- Bellarmine University: "Ultimate Questions"

- Brooklyn College: "Workplace Values and Happiness"

- Ithaca College: "Communication and the Human Spirit" (Communications/Media Studies) and "Cultivating Meditative Awareness" (Theatre)

- Kansas State University: "Spirituality & Leadership" (Leadership Studies)

- Mississippi State University: "Spirituality in Counseling" (Education)

- Montreat College: "Spiritual Formation and Faith Development" course which culminates in a retreat experience

- Mount Aloysius College: "The Self and Beyond: Psychology and Spirituality" (Psychology)

- North Park University: "Dialogue" (General Education/Writing Program)

- Peace College: "Adventures in Life and Learning"

- University of Arizona: "Values, Consciousness, and Higher Education"

- University of California at Berkeley: "Why Are We Here: Great Writing on the Meaning of Life"

- University of Iowa: "Mindfulness: Being Here With It All"

Spirituality and Wellness

Some faculty-led courses include practices that promote spirituality within the context of wellness. Often these courses engage students in contemplative practices. Examples include:

- American University presents a course on the practice of yoga and meditation. It is taught as a seminar and includes opportunities for hiking through neighboring parks and other field experiences. American University also offers a social justice and religion course that involves probing the deeper meaning of spirituality and spiritual practice.

- Southern Arkansas University offers a course called "Personal & Community Health," in which students are expected to "demonstrate knowledge of growth and development characteristics as they affect the physical, social, mental, intellectual, and spiritual aspects of holistic health."

- UCLA developed "Life Skills for College Women and Men," sponsored by Student Development and Health Education and based in the Department of Community Health Sciences. The course engages students on topics in three general areas: (1) stress, relaxation, and cognitive theory; (2) identity development; and (3) communication and relationships. Students fill out a weekly experience log that allows them to reflect, journal, and make meaning of the classroom exercises and conversations.

Other courses related to spirituality and wellness:

- University of Louisiana, Lafayette: "Exploring the Spiritual Experience in the Twelve Step Program of Alcoholics"

- Utica College: "Care of the Human Spirit" (Health Studies)

- Warner University: "Spiritual Practices" a class that deals with classic spiritual disciplines and ancient practices

Religious Studies Courses and Departments

Many campuses have Religious Studies Departments that offer baccalaureate degrees. Many also provide opportunities for students to take courses in theology, religious studies, or philosophy. Some examples:

- Brescia University offers a course called Faith and Justice in which students examine how a concern for social, economic, and political justice is rooted in the Gospel and mission of the Christian church. The course

presents the problem of structural injustice and strategies for alterna-
tives. Issues studied include human rights, abortion, poverty, hunger,
racism, sexism, pollution, and war.

- At University of Oklahoma–Norman Campus, the Religious Studies Program
  brings in speakers each semester for the entire community. Speakers
  who have participated include: Dr. Phillip Jenkins of Pennsylvania
  State University (The Next Christendom: The Coming of Global Christianity);
  Dr. Akbar Ahmed, Britain's Ambassador to Pakistan and Ibn Khaldun
  Professor of Islamic Studies at American University (Islam Under Siege:
  An Invitation to Interfaith Dialogue); Rabbi Bradley Hirschfield of the Jewish
  Center for Learning and Leadership (CLAL) (When God Goes to War);
  and Dr. Charles Kimball, Chair of the Department of Religious Studies
  at Wake Forest University (and author of When Religion Becomes Evil).
  The Outreach Program within the Religious Studies Program partici-
  pates in interfaith dialogue within the region and finally, students can
  participate in interfaith dialogue within the region through Religious
  Studies' Outreach Program.

- University of Wisconsin-Eau Claire offers a major or minor in religious studies
  along with general courses in the discipline to help fulfill their liberal
  arts, general education requirements. One sophomore-level course is
  titled "Sacred Earth: Religion & Nature," which "explores the historical,
  cultural, religious, and spiritual concerns of humanity's relationship
  with 'Nature' and environments, converging varieties or cultural expres-
  sions of the "sacred earth" in religious traditions, contemporary society,
  environmentalism, and science."

- Whittier College has a Buddhism class that is taught in a classroom
  setting during the semester and at a local monastery during an inten-
  sive winter session. The "immersion" at the monastery is usually 10
  days, with Buddhist monks leading meditation and preparing meals.
  The professor offers insight and instruction related to the history and
  practices of Buddhism, and support for students who are struggling
  with the experience.

Other similar campus courses or departments:

- Bethany College: "Peer Ministry" class

- Fayetteville State University: courses in religious traditions and sociology of religion

- Georgetown College: "Religion and Politics," "Religion and Popular Culture," "Religions of the Modern World," "Advanced Topics in World Religions," and "Religion and Violence"

- Guilford College: "Sacred Images, Altars and Rituals" (Art)

- Prescott College: "World Religions," "Mysticism," "Studies in Buddhism," "Religious Ethics and Environmental Activism," "Gender, Sexuality, and Religion," "Religion and Science," "Globalization, Religion and Social Change," and "Life Centering and Yoga: Philosophy and Practice." Contemplative practices are used throughout these courses.

- University of Kentucky: classes on spiritual differences and comparative religions (Anthropology), classes that explore life's meaning and purpose (Philosophy, Anthropology, Sociology, Psychology, History, and Geography). The University has Hebrew and Judaic Studies as well as a Catholic Studies Program.

TEACHING METHODS: STRATEGIES FOR FACILITATING SPIRITUAL DEVELOPMENT

In addition to formal academic programs and courses, there are a variety of teaching methods that faculty can employ to facilitate students' spiritual development. Collaboration between faculty from different disciplines to incorporate different approaches to teaching and learning, or to make cross-disciplinary connections between material, can encourage students to develop more integrated worldviews. Faculty at many campuses such as Evergreen State College and Queens University of Charlotte make links between philosophy, ethics, arts, religion, and related topics.

Faculty shared a variety of approaches to incorporating reflective writing or journaling exercises into undergraduate courses. Reflection facilitates deeper thinking about what students are learning, how their actions reflect their values, and so forth. Contemplative practices, such as moments of silence before or during class, can also help students take a step back from their busy lives. Faculty shared various teaching strategies, such as reflective writing, journaling, and related contemplative practices, including:

- Many faculty at **Biola University** assign "soul projects" where students are asked to examine how the material illuminates their own journey of spiritual and character development. These projects also allow for times of extended prayer and reflection, sometimes in solitude, other times in small groups.

- **Lesley University's "Spirituality: Psychological Resource for Individual and Social Well-Being"** includes a significant amount of self-reflective learning for students, through which they explore questions of meaning and purpose, employ contemplative practices, and learn about world religions.

- **Monmouth College** has a junior year general education requirement, **Reflections**, in which questions of ultimate meaning are explored from a variety of interdisciplinary perspectives. Reflections faculty have found that course assignments that foster contemplation, whether they be periods of silence or technology-free periods, are very effective and well-received by students.

- The chaplain and director of religious life community at **Simpson College** encourages moments of silence before teaching courses to encourage students to become fully present for the class. Students use this time to meditate, be still, and pray in their own faith traditions.

Other examples of contemplative practices in the classroom:

- Incorporating meditation, mindfulness or other contemplative practices into classes (**Antioch University of New England, Cornell College–Iowa, Hamline University**).

- Beginning classes with a moment of silent reflection (**Alvernia University, Louisiana Tech University**). Faculty at some religious campuses begin class with a prayer (**Molloy College**).

- Offering a "Meaning of Life" course developed by a professor of philosophy and religion and the campus chaplain, which requires a great deal of writing about how others have defined a meaningful life as well as how the students see life (Lincoln Memorial University).

- Beginning class with a bow. The bow symbolizes three parts: first, "sit up," to be aware of one's surroundings and become present; second, "feel," noticing one's inner experience and feeling one's body and heartbeat; and third, "give," bowing to honor others in the room and commit to being awake and present to what transpires during class (Naropa University).

CO-CURRICULAR PROGRAMS AND SERVICES

In addition to academic initiatives, academic affairs personnel and student affairs professionals have developed co-curricular programs and services designed to support students' spiritual growth. These practices encourage students to explore their spiritual identities and can help them gain insights about themselves that may be important to their search for meaning and purpose—what we refer to as Spiritual Quest. Initiatives that broaden students' experiences or expose students to the challenges that fellow human beings face can help students increase their levels of Ecumenical Worldview and Ethic of Caring. Efforts to support students through personal crises can help them learn to find appropriate mechanisms for dealing with emotional struggles and perhaps increase their long-term ability to achieve Equanimity.

In this section, rather than providing a comprehensive listing, we have selected examples to illustrate the range of programs and services we received. Co-curricular programs and services are grouped into the following sub-sections: *Awareness Weeks and Events; Spiritual Mentoring; Caring and Compassion for Others; Service and Immersion Programs; Encouraging a Search for Vocation; Dialogues About Spirituality and Religion; Meditation, Reflection, and Retreats; General Wellness; Student Leadership Training and Governance.*

AWARENESS WEEKS AND EVENTS

Some campuses hold special theme weeks or days to engage students in conversations about varied conceptions of spirituality and faith-based beliefs. At religious campuses, these weeks may frame spirituality in terms of the religious affiliation of the institution. Some examples include:

- Franklin College hosts a religious emphasis week each year, challenging students to focus on different faith issues and experiences. Franklin provides students with a labyrinth workshop each year, a way of teaching students to meditate and pray by utilizing the tools of pilgrimage, breathing, and walking. The campus provides continual programming that addresses the sense of caring and compassion for others, beginning the first day after students arrive on campus with a program called "Focus." The morning after new students arrive, they are led by two upper-class student peers, a faculty member, and a staff member to engage in some form of community service.

- Lawrence Technological University holds campus-wide celebrations for Eid, Diwali, Chinese New Year, Holy Thursday, and so forth. Events include reflective teaching with a spiritual leader, a dinner, and celebration.

- Montclair State University has experienced an increasing interest in spiritual life and, in response, different campus groups have collaborated to develop related programming. The university's Bonner students create a yearly (U.S.) Constitution Day, when freedom of speech and religious expression are discussed. They also have discussion and support groups for LGBTQ students, such as their Acceptance in Christ group, and LGBT discussion panels such as "For the Bible Tells Me So." Muslim students have a Jesus Awareness Day that is hosted with several Christian groups. Montclair also has Jewish-feminist seders during Passover. During Geek Week, there is "Bible geek" programming, which explores spiritual passion and curiosity. Finally, the campus teaches stress management, guided imagery, and meditation on an ongoing basis, and holds "Mind, Body, and Soul" fairs at the Recreation Center.

- At **Vassar College**, with the support of the Tanenbaum Inter-Religious Fellow at the College, the Office of Religious and Spiritual Life sponsors both a fall "coffee house" and a spring day to consider and celebrate "the role of religious and spiritual life" in a secular liberal arts education. Interfaith dialogue is sponsored through leadership development for student religious leaders, and the inter-religious council.

Other approaches to hosting awareness weeks or events:

- Many campuses devote one or more days or weeks to spirituality as a theme, each framing the purpose of the week differently. Some indicate a goal is spiritual emphasis, while others focus on "awareness," "development," "deepening," or "enrichment." Others seek to promote caring and compassion while still others may provide opportunities for spiritual direction with vocation directors. (**Asbury University, Calvin College, God's Bible School and College, Johnson Bible College, Malone University, Mid-Atlantic Christian University, Moody Bible Institute, Mount Mary College, Palm Beach Atlantic University, Shepherd University, Trevecca Nazarene University**). **Hannibal-LaGrange College** even hosts a spiritual life conference every semester.

- Other campuses promote interfaith dialogue or provide students with opportunities to learn about different religions through belief fairs, "interfaith expos," or religious emphasis weeks and other events (**The College of Saint Rose, Colorado College, Grambling State University, Grand Valley State University, Haverford College, Huston-Tillotson University, Maryville University, Paine College, Rosemont College, Saint Xavier University, Tennessee Tech University, University of Rhode Island, Villanova University**). **California State University, San Bernardino** facilitates interfaith dialogues through community service projects.

- Finally, some campuses offer programming that examines the intersections of spirituality, religion, or faith with culture (**King College's** Buechner Institute, **Geneva College's** Faith and Culture Week), race (**Martin Methodist College's** Convocation on Religion and Race), or other contemporary concerns (**Hastings College's** Religion in Life Week; **SUNY Geneseo's** Cultural Harmony Week).

SPIRITUAL MENTORING

At many campuses, educators have developed mechanisms for mentoring students' spiritually. Role-modeling the importance that many individuals place on their spiritual lives can facilitate students' own searches for meaning and purpose. For example:

- Tuesday Talks at Hendrix College are organized by the Miller Center and the Chaplain's Office, and have become a way for individuals from across all segments of the community—faculty, staff, administrators, and students—to explore spirituality, meaning, and purpose. Each Tuesday, a faculty or staff member is invited to speak at the noon hour on the question, "What is my calling and how do I know?"

- Cardinal Stritch University holds Mystic Pizza, an ecumenical gathering that is offered the first Wednesday evening of each month. Faculty and staff are invited to share stories with students of someone who has inspired them on their faith journey in life. The talk is followed by time for questions, conversation, and pizza.

- Monmouth College began a monthly series called "Why Am I Here? The Unfolding of Life," where faculty and staff talk about their personal lives and tell stories that help students understand that life does not always go in the direction one may expect.

- Nyack College has a Campus Mentor Team consisting of 10 faculty and staff families that live on campus. One goal is for these families to engage with students in their homes to discuss meaning, purpose, and issues related to students' spiritual development.

- Texas Christian University has a program called What Matters to Me and Why. According to TCU's website, the program is a monthly luncheon series where participants get a deeper, more personal look into the lives of faculty and staff members, specifically what they believe, why they believe it, and what motivates them.

- At William Jessup University, faculty and staff serve as leaders of small groups focused on students' spiritual formation.

CARING AND COMPASSION FOR OTHERS

Many campuses already offer students opportunities to engage with their local and global communities through direct service, service learning, or immersion programs. Some campuses such as Alma College and Gannon University include the campus community in their efforts to promote caring and compassion. Both institutions hold random-acts-of-kindness campaigns. Other campuses host programs and discussions such as "Soup and Substance" that encourage students to deeply explore issues, such as homelessness, which may only be solved when communities work together (Cal Poly State University, San Luis Obispo; Saint Peter's College). Still others develop innovative ways to encourage and support students' sense of caring toward others. Below are some examples of these practices:

- Hendrix College has an engaged learning requirement under a program called "Your Hendrix Odyssey." The faculty have recognized six categories of engaged learning: Service to the World, Professional and Leadership Development, Global Awareness, Artistic Creativity, Undergraduate Research, and Special Projects. Students must complete three projects from three different categories. Faculty or staff work with the student to design a service project with particular learning goals. These goals can be disciplinary-specific or oriented toward the "big questions." The student completes written- and oral-reflection components through which he or she connects the service work to ethical, intellectual, and personal-development questions.

- Mercer University offers Mercer on Mission (MOM), an international program that blends service and study, and aims to create a dynamic, life-changing synergism for students. MOM has elements of both a traditional study abroad program and a traditional service trip. The combination of study and service is designed to produce an increased understanding of a place and an increased investment in its people. To maximize the spiritual impact of this program, students keep a daily journal and respond to prompts that invite spiritual reflection.

- West Texas A&M University hosts Shack A Thon, a student-initated project. Hundreds of students build shacks and live in them. The initiative raises about $25,000 annually. All proceeds go to an entity that provides goats to refugees in Africa.

SERVICE AND IMMERSION PROGRAMS

Creating opportunities for students to engage in meaningful local, regional, national, and international service projects or to gain first-hand experience of other people's daily lives can facilitate spiritual development. Service experiences may promote spiritual qualities such as **Charitable Involvement**, **Ethic of Caring**, and **Ecumenical Worldview**. Service learning opportunities—which combine service with academic and reflective components and are so widespread that we did not discuss them in this guidebook—can promote **Spiritual Quest** in addition to the aforementioned qualities. Finally, immersion experiences, which are distinct from service experiences, are designed to broaden students' sense of community, thereby promoting a sense of solidarity with others. All of these experiences also serve to promote spiritual development. Examples include the following:

- Some campuses provide opportunities for students to voluntarily engage with local and international communities (**Chowan University's** Chowan Cares; **Davidson College's** Engage for Change; **Dallas Christian College's** Day of Service; **Eastern Michigan University's** alternative spring break opportunities and Volunteers in Service to Their Neighborhoods (VISION); **Daemen College's** food and clothing drives throughout the year and fundraising for Hospice Buffalo; **LeTourneau University's** S.T.U.D.S. (STUdents Devoted to Serve) and S.H.A.R.E (Students Helping Area Residents Excel). Other campuses require students to engage in community service (**Gallaudet University, Southwestern Christian University**). Finally, some campuses require student groups or athletic teams to fulfill service requirements (**Dakota Wesleyan University**).

- Alternative spring break service programs, where students engage in direct service to a community and participate in a reflective component to help process their experiences, may promote caring and compassion for others. Some campuses devote a great deal of time to preparing students for such week-long service trips that can be either local or international. **King's College** focuses its service trips on one theme, such as immigration or rural poverty. Students meet for six weeks in preparation for the experience, reflect daily, and participate in a follow-up meeting after the trip.

- Other institutionally sponsored experiences focus on helping students learn about another community (domestic or international) and come to an understanding of how that community lives. Such so-called immersion programs are hosted at many campuses including **Saint Joseph's University** (programs in Appalachia, the Gulf Coast, a Navajo reservation in New Mexico, Guatemala, Ecuador, and El Salvador). **Santa Clara University's Kolvenbach Solidarity Program** is primarily a co-curricular program, although some experiences are more curricular in nature. The program provides students with opportunities to learn with and from communities throughout the United States and Latin America. Through immersion, students come to understand what it means to live in solidarity with local and global communities. The program is founded on the principles of justice, community, spirituality, and simplicity. Groups of 10 -14 students meet weekly for five weeks of preparation, followed by several post-immersion gatherings, which integrate structured and non-structured opportunities for reflection.

- Through **Seattle University's Social Justice Ministry**, many opportunities abound for students to gain a sense of caring or compassion. Ministry service immersion opportunities challenge students to exercise compassion, social analysis, and faith reflection in experiencing developing-world conditions, while part of a community of learners. These experiences require an active commitment to faith, service, social justice, and building community. Participants pursue global issues of faith and justice in a community.

Other examples of service or immersion experiences:

- **Atlanta Christian College:** academic programs are closed once each semester and students are encouraged to participate in a ministry day.

- **Bloomsburg University of Pennsylvania:** The SOLVE office coordinates student volunteers with needs in the community.

- **CalArts** sends a group of students and faculty to work on the genocide project in Rwanda each summer.

- Cal Poly State University, San Luis Obispo has an "I Respect" program as part of its Student Community Services area. The campus also runs a program called "Soup and Substance," which has several topics each quarter dealing with global issues as well as local concerns such as homelessness.

- Gannon University hosts a program called "Pizza with a Purpose," a series of discussion groups led by the Social Concern Office. Previous topics have included: "American Politics and the Need for Civility " and " Cultural Responses to 9/11."

ENCOURAGING A SEARCH FOR VOCATION

Student affairs professionals and faculty can help students make connections between their personal values and their career choices. Career counselors are well versed in the many professional paths students can pursue based on their interests, skills, strengths, and personal calling. Faculty can facilitate class discussions about ways to use knowledge within their field to help their communities. By initiating conversations about students' life plans, student affairs professionals and faculty can challenge and support students' searches for meaning and purpose. Examples are:

- Bellarmine University's Career Development Center works with the Office of Campus Ministry to sponsor regular programs that ask, "What is God calling me to do?"—an approach to vocational discernment using spiritual practices and psychological inventories.

- Goshen College has a three-month summer offering called Inquiry Program through which students receive a summer stipend and tuition scholarship to explore "big questions" related to faith and vocation. Before, during, and after the summer session, students write reflection papers and participate in topically pertinent discussions.

- John Carroll University's "Senior Conversations" is a three-part conversation series that engages seniors in meaningful, small-group discussions co-hosted by a senior student and a faculty member. Each session focuses on one of the "Three Key Questions:" What brings you joy? What are you good at? Who needs you to do these things? The program offers a relaxed and social environment where seniors develop the tools necessary to engage in the process of discernment as well as a space where they can share their fears and anxieties about the uncertainty of life after graduation.

- Smith College houses a Center for Work and Life that promotes habits of reflection and integration of work preparation, wellness, leadership, and academics. Emphasis is placed on being thoughtful about one's "good life," or life well-lived. The Center's signature program is the Women's Narratives Project which brings students together to think about the meanings of success and a good life.

- Trinity Lutheran College's first-year experience offers a two-semester course called Vocation and Formation, in which students explore multiple spiritual practices and experiment with these in the classroom. The course weaves together journaling about spiritual practices, along with exercises and readings designed to uncover each student's sense of vocation.

- University of San Diego offers a Senior Get-Away Retreat, which encourages students to consider the issues of meaning, purpose, and spirituality. Initially a joint effort between Student Affairs, Career Services, and University Ministry, the retreat was designed to help seniors reflect on what they learned during college, where they found meaning and purpose, and how they could build futures that align with who they are and what they most deeply want.

Other practices that encourage vocational discernment include:

- Georgetown College: Philosophy course called "Discovering Vocation"

- Greensboro College: The First-Year Seminar Course explores the meaning and purposes of vocation and life, which also includes contemplative and discernment practices.

- Grove City College: An annual three-day Missions Conference gives students an opportunity to talk with more than 20 missions agencies about ministry opportunities.

- Loyola University of Chicago: The Personal Growth/Spiritual Development Program is designed to assist students in their ongoing personal growth and spiritual development along with their professional and vocational pursuits.

- Nebraska Methodist College: The college presents a seminar titled "Uncovering and Discovering Your Spiritual Path."

- Seton Hall University: Christian Employment Outreach, which is part of the Institute for Christian Spirituality, offers workshops that focus on discovering the spiritual dimension of work. The main focus is to help undergraduates understand and discover a religious and spiritual dimension to their everyday lives.

DIALOGUES ABOUT SPIRITUALITY AND RELIGION

Many campuses provide opportunities for students to engage in dialogue about spirituality and religion. Some programs focus solely on spirituality or religion, others address the intersection of the two, and still others are concerned primarily with interfaith understanding. Ultimately, many programs have the potential to build bridges across differences and cultivate an appreciation for a rich diversity of beliefs and perspectives.

Dialogues About Spirituality

Many campuses host a variety of forums that encourage dialogue about the intersections between spirituality and contemporary issues. Examples:

- Bates College supports students who consider themselves "Spiritual but not Religious," or even thoroughly secular, but who are looking for a place to talk about deep questions of meaning and purpose. The college holds biweekly dinners at the chaplain's home to discuss such questions and gather for casual conversation. Bates also has hosted a series of lectures called "Spirituali-Tea," which has prompted monthly conversations about the intersections of religion, spirituality, ethics, and politics.

- Saint Peter's College offers numerous opportunities for spiritual growth. The college hosts a program called "Soup and Substance," a brown-bag short presentation and conversation about spirituality and life, personally directed or weekend retreats designed around various spiritual themes, and spiritual direction for members of the campus community.

- University of Illinois (Urbana-Champaign) offers a Program on Intergroup Relations (PIR), sponsored by the Office on Inclusion and Intercultural Relations within student affairs. The program engages students in small-group classroom dialogues and reflective practices around issues of faith, belief, values, morality, and society in light of religious traditions and spiritual practices. As one of many PIR courses, this dialogue stimulates critical conversations around spiritual issues in the context of various other social-identity factors. It seeks to prepare students to explore and reflect on their own and others' perspectives in order to work and live in a diverse society and global marketplace.

- University of Southern California has a lecture series called "What Matters to Me and Why." The entire USC community is invited to engage as a way to pursue questions of meaning, purpose, and identity. The series encourages reflection about values, beliefs, and motivations, and helps students better understand the lives and inspirations of prominent figures within the university.

- University of Tampa has a "Spiritual Life through Film" series, screening movies that relate to character-building, spiritual development, and greater understanding of world cultures and religions. After the film presentation, a faculty panel discusses these themes and analyzes the film with the students.

- University of Virginia offers "Sustained Dialogue," a student-run group that conducts dialogue on issues of prejudice and bias within the community. Organizers form small groups at the beginning of the year that meet weekly and use teaching methods developed at Princeton to address conflict in the Middle East. In addition, the University's religiously affiliated groups (more than 50) discuss "big questions." The discussions take many forms, such as Bible study and close reading of the Torah and the Koran, and are held at various places, including Hillel and the Tibetan cultural center.

Examples of dialogue-based spirituality programming at other campuses:

- Beloit College has a weekly small-group experience called "Live the Questions."

- Fairfield University has adopted the residential college model for sophomore year, designed to have students ask life's larger questions and embrace taking responsibility for the broader community.

- Fisher College hosts a weekly "Spiritual Explorations" workshop.

- Lubbock Christian University: The Student Involvement Office works with other campus groups to create co-curricular programming around Christian higher education to address various student needs. Programs, such as the "Sex, Singleness, and Spirituality" forum, ask students: "How does my faith speak to this particular issue or problem?"

- Southern Vermont College is not a faith-based college, but together with Bennington's Interfaith Council clergy the college sets up a "roving clergy" series that addresses spirituality topics, and provides opportunities for spiritual counseling.

- Stetson University's "Fridays at 4" is a model for students to gather and discuss in an open, welcoming, and inclusive environment, issues that are timely and/or provocative.

- Wilson College: Chaplaincy-run program called "Big Questions" that brings in community members to present and discuss what gives meaning to their lives

- Universidad del Este (Puerto Rico) offers Moment of Reflection, a short dialogue about topics related to spiritual practice and how to apply it in daily life.

- University of North Texas: The Dean of Students and Equity and Diversity Offices collaborate on opportunities for students to explore their spiritual development.

Religious Dialogues

Religious and non-religious campuses alike provide students with a range of opportunities to learn more about various religious traditions or to enhance their religious lives. For instance, Bethel University, provides multiple opportunities for religious and spiritual life enhancement through the residence halls, campus ministries, and leadership in Christian ministries. Regular chapel services are also available at Bethel and many other campuses (e.g., Cincinnati Christian University, College of Mount St. Joseph, Heritage Christian University, Maranatha Baptist Bible College, MidAmerica Nazarene University, Taylor University, Wittenberg University).

Other campuses merge conversations about faith with discussions about contemporary issues. "Theology on Tap" is a popular program that varies by campus. At Loyola Marymount University, for example, invited speakers with an expertise in a specific area of theology or spirituality give a short talk followed by a conversation about the topic. At Bucknell University, students talk about current issues at a local pub. At Pennsylvania State University-Mont Alto, participants have the opportunity to explore a variety of religions, faiths, spiritualities, and celebrations.

Other practices designed to facilitate religious dialogues or help students enhance their religious lives:

- Princeton University's Religious Life Council (RLC) brings dialogue about religious pluralism to the core of campus conversations. Made up of a dynamic group of undergraduate and graduate students from more than 10 different faith traditions as well as religiously unaffiliated members, the RLC is committed to fostering conversation between all religious faiths at Princeton as well as at the national and international level. Weekly roundtable discussions include topics such as religion and art, conversion, modesty, and the death penalty. The RLC also collaborates with the residential colleges and other centers and academic offices on campus to encourage student participation in discussion about religion at Princeton.

- Rochester College has a student-led initiative called the "House of God" series. It brings sensitive or controversial issues into open dialogue between known interfaith or non-faith proponents who are active around the greater-Detroit metropolitan area. This dialogue, which is open to the whole campus and the surrounding community, is reported to provide a wonderful exploration of faiths and culture.

- **University of Missouri's** Muslim Student Organization and Jewish Student Organization have sponsored dialogues on the Gaza settlements. They also have an association of **Campus Religious Advisors** that meets monthly. The association consists of staff from the student ministry programs that are sponsored by various community churches.

- **Yale University** has a **Multi-Faith Council** of self-selected students from different faith traditions who meet weekly for dinner and discussion. This Council sponsors campus-wide religious awareness activities. An **Interreligious Leadership Council** of student leaders from different religious organizations also meets biweekly.

Student religious groups at both religious and non-religious campuses often provide settings for students to dialogue about religion. For instance, **Rowan University** hosts several religious student groups: Chi Alpha, Fellowship of Christian Athletes, Hillel, New Life Ministry, Catholic Campus Ministry and Rowan Christian Fellowship. Another example is **Southern Illinois University–Carbondale**, which has 12 faith-based student organizations and an active campus ministry. At campuses such as **Indiana University–Purdue University Fort Wayne**, the many faith-based student organizations also convene as an interfaith council.

At religious and non-religious campuses alike, Campus Ministry departments, often with the help of student boards, frequently take responsibility for coordinating various religious activities. The **College of Notre Dame of Maryland** has a student board within Campus Ministry that hosts co-curricular religious activities, including prayer groups, trips to various churches and mosques, annual Jewish seders, Christian songfests, Tenebrae service, and interfaith Advent prayer services. Similarly, **Silver Lake College of the Holy Family** focuses on religious and spiritual aspects of students' education, and has programming that addresses life's "big questions" through small faith-sharing groups. Campus Ministry departments frequently offer programming specifically designed to promote interfaith dialogue (see next sub-section).

Additional examples of practices that promote religious dialogue and provide students with ways to enhance their religious lives:

- Centre College hosts CentreFaith, which presents films on campus, and is co-sponsored by the Jewish Student Organization or the Muslim Student Association. The college also organizes special events centered around the religious holidays of various traditions.

- Olivet Nazarene University offers prayer groups, "Party with Jesus" (a student-led worship service), ministry groups that travel, and partnerships with community organizations.

- Roberts Wesleyan College offers "Faith Integration Fridays," which are not worship services, but rather dialogue-oriented. Examples include: a dramatic play addressing a theme, followed by break-out groups for discussion; a video of an organization helping AIDS victims, followed by physically packing AIDS Workers' health kits; an ecological topic followed by an outdoor activity; or visits to senior communities for life-sharing during a coffee break.

- University of Dayton presents Perspectives on Faith and Life Series, which consists of dinner, discussion, and speakers who facilitate dialogue among students, faculty, and staff about religious beliefs as they relate to various academic disciplines.

- Wiley College has a weekly religious service that is mandatory for all students except seniors. Worship is led by ministers of various Christian denominations. Dialogues are conducted with students and faculty of non-Christian religions.

Interfaith Dialogues

Like the dialogues about spirituality and religion discussed above, interfaith dialogues have the potential to promote students' understanding and respect for other spiritual and religious traditions.

- Allegheny College hosts an Interfaith Fellowship (IFF) that coordinates interfaith dialogues and events such as Faith Week, which explores religion and social change, spiritual health, and religion as a motivation for community service. With the campus becoming more diverse, the chaplain works with the wellness committee, environmental groups, and various student affairs groups to provide opportunities for student reflection on the spiritual dimension of vocational, economic, and political choices, and ethical issues that arise.

• **Fisk University's Leaders of the Interfaith Fellowship Team** (L.I.F.T.) seek to: 1) provide a forum for dialogue among students who are both leaders and representatives of religious denominations or organizations, 2) enhance the religious life of all students, 3) promote tolerance and acceptance of the variety of different religious perspectives, and 4) promote interfaith activities (e.g., worship services and panel discussions) that stimulate both critical and analytical discussions about issues affecting humanity (e.g., poverty, violence, and world hunger). L.I.F.T. includes the Fisk Memorial Chapel Assistants, The Wesley Foundation at Fisk University, the Mount Zion College Ministry, Young Excited and Saved (Y.E.S.) Ministries, Every Nation Campus Ministries, and the Fellowship of Christian Athletes.

• **Florida State University (FSU)** has an active campus ministry council that coordinates and publicizes the individual and collaborative events of 30 religious and spiritual campus groups. The activities include Engage Your World Interfaith Dialogue, Middle East Center speaker series, and the FSU Spiritual Life Project workshops and roundtables. **The FSU Spiritual Life Project** has embarked on a journey of encouraging and discovering ways to facilitate students' spiritual development with faculty, staff, and other students across campus.

Many campuses have multi-faith groups, interfaith alliances, inter-religious councils, or similar variations. The purpose of some groups is to provide a venue for interfaith discussion and faith sharing. Other groups, which may consist of student leaders from various student religious organizations, develop programming to enrich campus opportunities for fellowship. Still others may sponsor interfaith dialogues to educate students about different faiths or to promote interfaith discussions. Campuses vary in the degree to which they provide administrative and financial support for these groups. Examples of campuses that have these types of groups include Alma College, Avila University, Berry College, Campbell University, 12 campuses in the Cleveland area that are served by the Cleveland Hillel Foundation, Cheyney University of Pennsylvania, Eastern Connecticut State University, Gettysburg College, and St. Bonaventure University.

Finally, many colleges and universities provide opportunities for interfaith spiritual practices (e.g. SUNY Maritime College) or have formal, organized interfaith discussions and prayer services (e.g. Susquehanna University, Vaughn College).

Additional examples of interfaith dialogue include:

- College of Mount Saint Vincent: "Faith" discussions always include a panel composed of students from various faith traditions.

- Lebanon Valley College: "Sustained Dialogues" include interfaith topics. Each semester, the college hosts an interfaith banquet introducing students to traditions, music, dance, and food of a different faith tradition.

- Massachusetts Institute of Technology: The Addir Fellows program brings together more than 30 students each year to learn about the religious traditions of their classmates.

- Miles College: Sponsors an annual Interfaith Prayer Service, "The Community in Prayer," in which persons of different faith traditions share prayers and readings from their tradition.

- Mills College: The college presents Interfaith Youth Core Workshops for students and faculty.

- Oklahoma City University: A non-denominational chapel is held weekly, and interfaith dialogues with both Jewish- and Muslim-community faith representatives are presented several times each semester.

- Piedmont College: The college offers Religion 101 field trips to worship settings for various faith traditions, facilitating interfaith dialogue.

- **Tufts University:** The university supports CAFE (Conversations, Action, Faith and Education), a student group that works at fostering dialogue among all believers and non-believers

- **University of Houston-Downtown:** The university engages students in Inter-Religious Dialogue focused on understanding others through stories of various faith's teachings.

- **University of Massachusetts Lowell:** The university employs several ministers on campus who provide both regular and "special" opportunities for interfaith dialogue.

MEDITATION, REFLECTION, AND RETREATS

Numerous campuses offer students opportunities to experience formal retreats and other structured opportunites for students to engage in contemplative practices (e.g. Cabrini College, Carroll College). Campus Ministry departments also often house a variety of religious and non-religious retreats for students (e.g. Canisius College).

- **Bryn Athyn College** has "Sacred Space" time every day from 10:30-11 a.m., when everything shuts down, except for spiritual activities. No classes are scheduled during this time.

- During the summer, a psychology professor at **Cedar Crest College** gives talks outdoors on issues of meaning and purpose in people's lives. The series, called "Reflections Under the Trees," is open to the entire campus community.

- At **Conception Seminary College**, students have a number of **Days of Recol-lection** (silent retreats for one day) during which they hear short presentations by retreat masters, are silent for that day, and refrain from any internet use. The days (about one per month) are set aside for quiet reflection and private prayer.

- Each term, **Dominican University of California** offers a **Busy Person's Retreat**, providing faculty, staff, and students the opportunity to meet daily with a spiritual advisor to discuss a reading from Christian scripture or other book. Felician College also offers "busy person" retreats twice a year to faculty, staff, and students.

• George Mason University created a living-learning community called "Mindful Living" in one of the residential halls.

• The Office of the Dean of the Chapel at Indiana Wesleyan University hosts a "Still" event. "Stations" are set up around the chapel-auditorium, with each station asking participants to reflect on different issues. During the second week of the semester, the office hosts a week of special services called "Summit." These services are meant to spiritually renew the campus community. Invited speakers discuss different world religions and how Christians should be relating to them.

• Iona College holds a Kairos weekend, a popular retreat program that many campuses across the country offer. The weekend retreat is student-led, and engages students in reflection on and affirmation of their relationships with God, others, and themselves. Student leaders and professional staff "witness" talks and small-group break-out sessions designed to help promote personal insight, build a supportive community, and inspire active involvement and service. Monthly follow-up meetings, called "Fourth Day" sessions, foster on-going faith development and discovery.

• Pacific Lutheran University organizes the EXPLORE! retreat for first-year students, aimed at asking students to consider big questions around "the vocation of learning."

GENERAL WELLNESS

Spiritual development includes the development of internal mechanisms to be calm or centered during times of stress. Some campuses offer programming to help students learn to manage stress. These practices include:

• Nebraska Wesleyan University has several programs on campus designed to help students deal with stress, especially around finals times, with what they call "revival stations." Some are more spiritually oriented (prayer beads, yoga, etc.) and others are simply stress relief (good food, pet therapy, etc.).

• **Purchase College State University of New York** has a Wellness Center and a campus- wide Wellness Committee. One of the sub-committees is a **Spiritual Wellness Alliance**. They also offer yoga every day of the week and meditation twice a week.

• **Virginia Commonwealth University** holds stress-management workshops and curriculum-infusion workshops, and discusses the purpose and impact of prayer with students to present prayer as one strategy for health and stress management.

Many campuses already support students' general well-being by offering classes and workshops in meditation, yoga, and stress management (**Loyola College Maryland**), pastoral counseling (**College of Mount Saint Vincent**), or other formal counseling services (**Coastal Carolina University, Oregon Institute of Technology**). Additionally, many counseling centers conduct outreach programs, such as "**Check up from the Neck Up**," a depression screening held at **Pace University in New York**. **Concordia University Wisconsin**'s counseling services holds "**Faces of Depression**," a program that encourages students to share, through a number of creative ways, how they deal with pain or stress in life and how the arts and the campus community is helpful.

Other campus practices geared toward facilitating students' general wellness:

• **Earlham College** distributes weekly announcements about stress and coping skills in "**Around the Heart**," the college's electronic newsletter.

• At **Ferrum College**, the chaplain's office, the counseling center, and Resident Educators are trained to assist students to better cope with stress.

• **Missouri Southern State University** offers a wide variety of stress-reduction activities, such as time-managment workshops, study-habit workshops, test-taking tips, free massage appointments during finals, and social activities for students to take a break during mid-terms and finals.

- At Rivier College, the Nursing Department, Counseling Center, and Campus Ministry co-sponsor "Stress Relief Weeks" three times a year.

- Roosevelt University's Stress Management and Relaxation Training (SMART), a series of four group sessions, provides knowledge and stress management skills to improve success in students' personal life, college career, and beyond.

- Savannah State University offers grief counseling, along with wellness and healthy-living programs.

- The University of California at Santa Barbara has a Stress Management Peer Advisor program in the Stress Management Program Office (SMPO) of Counseling Services.

STUDENT LEADERSHIP TRAINING AND GOVERNANCE

Some campuses have developed creative ways to integrate spiritual development into existing student activities. One approach is to develop student leadership programs that focus on training students to become spiritual leaders who can minister to their peers. Another is to encourage existing associated student bodies or student governments to establish sub-committees or councils to focus on spiritual development. Or, campus committees or councils might invite students to represent the views of their peers on spiritual or religious matters. There are numerous ways for campuses to incorporate spiritual development into student leadership activities, including the following:

- DePaul University's Student Interfaith Scholars program develops a cohort of eight student leaders annually. They receive training and direct experience in interfaith learning and service, and then educate and engage their peers in similar opportunities.

- Kenyon College has developed a Spiritual Advisors Program, which encourages students to reexamine the moral, religious, and spiritual values they have held all of their lives. Spiritual Advisors aim to provide an ear and feedback to students struggling with spiritual questions of meaning and purpose. Advisors come from a diversity of faith backgrounds; some define themselves as seekers with no particular faith and are trained in listening skills, religious diversity, and active avoidance of anything that could be interpreted as proselytizing.

- **University of St. Thomas's Student Spirituality Committee** reflects a collaboration between Campus Ministry and the Undergraduate Student Government (USG). The purpose and intent of the committee (which is made up of students) is to engage all students in the exploration of and dialogue about spirituality. Events have included an evening of journaling, where the group, over dinner, explored best practices for spiritual journaling and reflection, and dialogue events with leaders of the major religious and spiritual traditions (Christianity, Islam, Judaism, Buddhism, and Hinduism). USG, in collaboration with the Campus Ministry, also developed the "Mind, Body, Spirit" campaign, designed to invite students to consider holistic development through engagement in suggested activities (service, prayer, meditation, etc.).

Additional examples of student leadership training and student organizations:

- **Asbury University's** student government has a branch dedicated to spiritual life that operates like a student activities board.

- **Austin College** has a **Service Station**, through which much of the student body participates in community service every year. The campus also has the **Activators Program**, engaging students in planning and leading youth ministry events connected to the Presbyterian Church.

- At **Bentley University**, student leadership training related to spiritual development takes many forms. Resident Assistant training sessions include workshops on inter-religious dialogue. **The Spiritual Life Center** has an Advisory Board that includes students, faculty, and staff. The Diversity Student Council includes representatives from the faith-based clubs: Catholic, Protestant, Jewish, and Muslim.

- In **Bridgewater College's Student Peer Ministry Program**, trained students offer caring and compassion to their peers.

- VisionQuest at Dillard University encourages students to explore life's big questions through The Leadership Institute, a series of three, seven-hour workshops that present life questions and allow students to direct their responses to each other.

- Jackson State University has more than 10 active religious organizations on campus, most of which are student-led and student-initiated. The university has an open policy on campus that permits any student, of any faith conviction, the freedom to start an organization for like-minded individuals on campus.

- All Neumann University student-athletes participate in an evening of reflection on a particular aspect of the values depicted on the five pillars in the atrium of the Mirenda Center for Sport Spirituality and Character Development: beauty, reflection, balance, play, and respect.

- Our Lady of the Lake University has a Providence Leadership Program that engages students in learning more about "call" and response," as well as the sponsoring congregation that started the university. The campus also has several core groups of students who serve as peer ministers for other students experiencing stress.

- Sam Houston State University has a student-led group called "One," which is sponsored and advised by the Dean of Students Office. The group's motto is "One key aspect of leadership is your spiritual walk. Great Leaders are servant leaders."

- Southern Oregon University's student-athletes participate in a Champions of Character Initiative.

- SUNY Potsdam's leadership programs invite student leaders to explore the "big questions" and to understand their own values, motivations, and ways of creating meaning.

- University of Southern Maine offers a course called "Ethical and Spiritual Dimensions of Leadership."

CAMPUS-WIDE EFFORTS

Effective promotion of campus efforts to facilitate students' spiritual development, as with many initiatives that prompt mixed reactions, requires leadership and collaboration. Administrators can provide critical leadership by communicating the institution's commitment to supporting students' spiritual development. The climate around spirituality will likely vary by campus, and clear communication can help faculty, student affairs professionals, and student leaders determine how best to engage in this work. The way in which administrators provide leadership in spiritual development can take many forms. Although space limitations prevent us from describing all the practices shared with us, we present a limited number of examples under the following headings: *Leadership and Strategic Planning; Campus Centers and Organizational Units; Residence Life Initiatives; First-Year Experience; University-Wide Initiatives; Faculty and Staff Development; Recognition and Rewards; Designated Physical Spaces; and Financial Support for Initiatives Relating to Spiritual Development.*

LEADERSHIP AND STRATEGIC PLANNING

Senior administrators may have the greatest influence over the direction a campus pursues in relation to its overall mission, but successful initiatives typically require the involvement of a broader range of individuals. Designating full-time positions or appointing committees and councils to focus specifically on issues of spirituality related to the entire campus can be effective in advancing this work. These groups can develop strategic plans for achieving any campus-wide spirituality goals.

Administrative Positions, Committees, and Councils

Campus leaders who are interested in developing or improving efforts to facilitate students' spiritual development can designate one or more positions to focus on spirituality; or they can appoint a small group of individuals to look at how spirituality can fit into campus life. These individuals might create a planning document that outlines concrete initiatives with specified measures of success.

- **Bard College** has formed a **Commission on Religion** that seeks to address the increasing influence of religion in world affairs, and the challenge this resurgence poses to the tradition and practice of a liberal arts education.

- **Belmont University** designates campus leaders to focus on spiritual development, including a vice president for spiritual development, a university minister, and two associate university ministers. They work with faculty, staff, and students in promoting ways to help students develop spiritually.

- **Middlebury College** has a **Religious Life Council** that meets monthly with representatives of 12 religious groups, including Intervarsity Christian Fellowship (Christian), Hillel (Jewish), Islamic Society, Unitarian Universalists, Christian Science, Prajna Meditation Society, and Newman Catholic Student Organization, among others. The college has held several religious life awareness weeks over the years, and twice has expanded to month-long awareness periods.

- On the first day of each month, the president of **Ouachita Baptist University** sends out to students, faculty, and staff, **"First Thoughts,"** a brief campus update that often includes reflections on topics related to spiritual development, such as gratitude, faith, growth, and so forth.

Other examples of campuses creating administrative positions focused on spiritual issues include **Cedarville University's** 14 full-time staff in the Christian Ministries Division; **Ohio Dominican University's** vice president for mission and identity; **Skidmore College's** director of spiritual life; and **The University of San Francisco's** full-time minister, whose responsibility is to further spiritual development and faith formation for people of all faith traditions.

Other examples of councils and committees with similar purposes include **College of the Holy Cross's** College Committee on Mission and Identity; **East Texas Baptist University's** Chapel Advisory Committee and Committee for the Integration of Faith and Learning; **Elon University's** academic standing committee for Religious and Spiritual Life; **Florida A&M University's** Campus Ministry Board; **North Greenville University's** Faith, Race, and Culture Committee; and **Southern Adventist University's** spiritual life committee.

Mission Statements and Strategic Plans
Endorsing the notion that supporting students' spiritual development is within the purview of colleges and universities might encourage involvement of a

broader range of constituents than normally might be involved in such work. Campus leaders could publicly signal their support for spiritual development work in mission statements; at campus events such as convocations; and in publications and media documents that inform and shape public perceptions of the institution, such as presidential and admissions websites. Examples of these approaches follow.

- **Centenary College of New Jersey** incorporates "questions of meaning and purpose" into institution-wide expected learning outcomes. Similarly, the division of Student Engagement and Development at **Immaculata University** adopted goals for learning outcomes that include objectives for encouraging students to explore their spiritual development.

- **Eastern University**'s mission encompasses faith, reason, and justice, and these themes are interwoven throughout students' experiences both inside and outside the classroom.

- **The University of Richmond** Office of the Chaplaincy recently completed a new strategic plan called "**Inspiring Generous Faith; Engaging the Heart of the University**." Two of the plan's five strategic objectives are to create opportunities for students to explore their own spiritual experiences and those of others, and to animate "conversations of meaning" that bring together people across many lines of difference, including sacred and secular differences.

- **Western Connecticut State University**'s strategic plan focuses on student engagement. One of the sub-goals stresses the importance of spiritual development as part of overall "wellness." The University has also established a wellness initiative that will include elements of spirituality in all of its dimensions.

Other examples of campuses with mission statements or plans that endorse the idea of supporting students' spiritual development:

- **Notre Dame College** is engaged in major efforts to encourage dialogue about student's spirituality as part of its strategic plan. They have begun to do this by offering the Freshman Seminar, which explores questions of meaning and purpose.

- Nyack College: The Office of Spiritual Formation has a mission statement for spiritual formation and program goals.

- Regent University: A quality-enhancement plan is titled "Developing Globally Competent Christian Leaders."

- Wartburg College: The mission statement expresses the institution's dedication "to challenging and nurturing students for lives of leadership and service as a spirited expression of their faith and learning. "

- William Jewell College: Its mission statement includes "spiritual growth."

CAMPUS CENTERS AND ORGANIZATIONAL UNITS

Campus leaders may support centralized efforts to promote interfaith dialogue, spirituality, service, and related intersections by demonstrating the value an institution places on spiritual development, thus indirectly facilitating students' spiritual development. For example:

- Hampshire College has both a Spiritual Life Office and a Center for Spiritual Life. The college's website explains that the Spiritual Life program "provides the space and support for spiritual exploration, development, and appreciation." Furthermore, these two units encourage: "healthy community life, interaction, and reconciliation across boundaries of ideas, possibilities, and faiths," and "offer support so that students, staff, and faculty can flourish and experience the connections between mind, body, and spirit, and a place where we can become fully ourselves even as we lift up and celebrate our diverse community."

- Maryville College's Center for Calling and Career has been developed to help students reflect on their own sense of meaning and purpose, and discover their talents in order to find their "calling" for the future. In addition, the capstone ethics class and the first-year seminar include a vocation unit, so students begin and end their time at the college considering questions of meaning, purpose, and value.

- **Oberlin College and Conservatory of Music's Office of Religious and Spiritual Life** is involved in a variety of programming, including: offering courses to encourage students' exploration of life's big questions; promoting global worldview and awareness weeks; prioritizing caring and compassion through justice projects; hosting a Friendship Day Festival that draws upon Islamic concepts of friendship and global peacemaking; offering lectures on atheism and the apocalypse; and hosting a variety of other events like Multi-faith Awareness Week.

- **Occidental College** has an **Office for Religious and Spiritual Life**, which provides leadership and resources for programs that explore spirituality, religion, ethics, moral development, social justice, religious diversity, and the pursuit of meaningful work. Funded through the Lilly Endowment, the office encourages students to engage with the big questions concerning truth, morality, religious beliefs, and meaning. Students can apply for Values and Vocations Fellowships to explore these types of spiritual questions. Values and Vocations retreats, service opportunities, and a variety of other projects focus on spiritual development.

- **Spelman College's WISDOM Center** provides guided meditation as a co-curricular activity, offered during the academic year by two faculty members. Interfaith dialogue also occurs within the center. And, the center has three student learning and development programs that focus on vocation, purpose, meaning, and faith. The Sisters Chapel has a prayer room used for multi-faith convening, prayer, quiet reflection, and meditation.

- **University of California, San Diego** houses a **Center for Ethics and Spirituality** that provides counseling, discussion, and education programs related to spiritual, moral, and ethical issues. The center also hosts quarterly lectures on issues related to ethics, spirituality, norms, and morality, as well as workshops that provide strategies for recognizing and avoiding cults and high-pressure recruitment.

Other campus centers:

- Ashland University: Center of Religious Life

- Barton College: Center for Faith and Spirituality

- Boston College: University Mission and Ministry

- Cardinal Stritch University: Center for Calling and Engagement

- Franklin Pierce University: Office of Interfaith Campus Ministries

- Gonzaga University: University Ministry Department

- Grinnell College: Center for Religion, Spirituality and Social Justice

- Lehigh University: Center for Dialogue, Ethics, and Spirituality

- Nazareth College: Center for Interfaith Study and Dialogue

- Springfield College: Spiritual Life Center

- University of New Hampshire: The Chaplains Association and the Waysmeet Center

- William Woods University: Office of Faith and Service

- Xavier University of Louisiana: Office of Campus Ministry

RESIDENCE LIFE INITIATIVES

Living-learning communities in campus housing can provide unique structures to support students' spiritual development. Examples include:

- Messiah College's Reconciliation House, a live-in residence for students, hosts a program called "Let Me Explain," which allows for discussion of differences in a safe and confidential environment.

- Regis University's Romero House consists of six students and one coordinator who live in "intentional community" for one academic year, and are dedicated to principles of simplicity, social justice, and spirituality.

- Rollins College's interfaith residential option is found in one of the residence halls.

- Westmont College's faculty members volunteer to host reading groups and forums in the residence halls that address themes of spiritual and intellectual development.

FIRST-YEAR EXPERIENCE

Many colleges already have an office or department that focuses on the well-being and success of first-year students. Although these units may not have a mission that is directly spiritual in nature, first-year experience programs have the potential to offer programming that encourages students to consider life's big questions from the very beginning of their college career.

Some first-year experience programs provide opportunities for spiritual development by introducing the Big Questions into their orientation programs (Cornerstone University's Terra Firma program; Eastern Oregon University's first-year program; Elmhurst College's Big Questions: What Will You Stand For?). Others promote caring and compassion (University of the Pacific's course, "What is a Good Society?"), or challenge students with the Big Questions in their first-year experience seminars (Hope College; Mississippi College).

Other first-year experience practices:

- DeSales University's Freshmen Character program helps student participants and leaders to deal with issues of stress and maturity.

- The Institute of American Indian Arts' freshman orientation includes a ropes course and specific team-building activities to promote community, caring, and mutual support. A weekly "Talking Circle" and potluck dinners continue this caring student community of mutual support.

- Juniata College's Church Search program is offered to incoming students, who are invited to gather on Sunday mornings during the first month of the fall semester to visit local churches. Each week they visit several churches and then reconvene after the visits for group reflection on the experience. The program encourages students to find a church home during college, and to meet and interact with students of other denominations early in their first year.

• Through the University of Great Falls's Corps of Discovery first-year experiential program, the university expects students to develop creeds; an understanding of personal commitment, interest and vocation; and an awareness of their responsibilities as members of communities.

UNIVERSITY-WIDE INITIATIVES

In addition to department and division-wide practices, many campuses are engaged in university-wide efforts to promote spiritual development:

• Miami University offered a year-long program on religion and community led by the Center for American and World Cultures. Campus initiatives aim to engage faculty and staff in conversations about how to address religious issues that may arise with students, develop residential learning communities focused on the themes of religion and spirituality, and create a multi-purpose space for reflection-meditation-prayer. Plans also include hosting a summer conference with educators at similar institutions. Conference participants would discuss ways to address tensions related to religious pluralism, and develop seminars about managing difficult classroom dialogues, such as when students present religious justifications for their beliefs.

• Hartwick College offers a month-long programming series called "Searching for Spirituality" through the Office of Interfaith and Spirituality. The series involves an Interfaith Fair, movie, and discussions with student organizations. It also includes panel discussions led by both faculty and community faith-based leaders on topics such as: "What it Means to Be Faithful," "Love & Marriage and Everything in Between," "What it Means to Be Christian," "Doubters vs. Non-Doubters," "What it Means to Be Atheist and Agnostic," "The Difference between Spirituality and Religion," and "Beyond the Afterlife: What Happens After Death."

• The Schuylkill campus of Pennsylvania State University has run a lecture series for 24 years on various philosophical and religious topics, guided by an annually selected theme. Themes have included Great Philosophers on Religion, Spirituality and Health, Great Figures in Christianity, the Presence of Religious Faith in America, and Religious Faith in Contemporary American Society. A faculty member is responsible for the lecture series and is assisted by student officers of the Religious and Philosophical Forum.

• University of Pittsburgh sponsors an Outside the Classroom Curriculum, a University-wide initiative designed to educate the whole student through completion of a series of programs, activities, and experiences that complement each student's academic studies. The curriculum engages students as they grow in nine key areas: leadership development, sense of self, career preparation, university participation, communication skills, respect for diversity, healthy lifestyles, service to others, and appreciation for the arts.

• Wilberforce University hosts an annual campus colloquium called "People of the Book," a dialogue between Judaism, Christianity and Islam. Other campus events include Men's Spiritual Empowerment Week; Women's Spiritual Empowerment Week; Bible studies, Meet the Chaplain Days; and Prayer Vigils.

Other campus efforts that involve broad-scale collaborations:

• Florida Southern College's Faith and Life Convocation series brings in speakers to explore topics that address life's "big questions."

• Marquette University's Manresa Project uses elements of Ignatian Spirituality in curricular and co-curricular settings to provide students with opportunities to think more seriously about the big questions of meaning and purpose, and their interrelationships with the global community. Faculty have reported that this experience transformed their teaching and helped them better connect academic content to students' life paths and overall development in college.

• Providence College's Office of the Chaplain/Campus Ministry and Center for Catholic and Dominican Studies offer extensive programs, lectures, and discussions. Recent topics include Jewish and Catholic perspectives on priesthood, the sexual-abuse crisis in the church, images of the feminine in Catholicism, perspectives on hell, chastity, and sexuality, and a series on various forms of prayer.

• **Trinity College's "The Mindfulness Project"** provides introductions for faculty, staff, and students to practices and traditions that foster personal centeredness and the integration of mind, body, and spirit.

FACULTY AND STAFF DEVELOPMENT

Campus administrators can indirectly support students' spiritual development through faculty and staff development activities. These activities can provide a venue for faculty and staff to develop their skills in working with students, or generate creative ideas for incorporating spiritual development into their work. Efforts might also involve support for faculty and staff spiritual development. Examples are below.

Orientation and Professional Development

During new faculty and staff orientations, campus administrators can communicate any campus-wide commitment to facilitating students' spiritual development. At religious campuses, like **St. John's University in New York**, for example, performance appraisals may take into account employees' efforts to pursue the institution's mission. Beyond orientation, follow-up programs can provide additional training for those faculty and staff interested in aligning their work with the campus' spiritual development goals.

• At **Butler University**, faculty and staff can learn to tune into the spiritual and religious questions and concerns of students, and their longing for purpose and meaning, through the Center for Faith and Vocation's annual **Workshop on Faith and the Vocation of Education**. Professors and staff can participate in the year-long workshop in which they reflect on their own sense of vocation, or calling, to work in education. Participants also learn how to enhance academic and other forms of student advising, as well as mentoring, to include questions and reflection on matters of faith and spirituality (where appropriate), and on discerning one's calling. They also learn about the reality of religious diversity on campus and hear first-hand from students about the place of religion in their lives. New faculty participate in a workshop offered by the Center for Faith and Vocation as part of the comprehensive new faculty development initiative of the associate provost for faculty and interdisciplinary programs.

- **Edgewood College** provides student affairs and faculty development by using a student affairs division retreat to promote the importance of student spiritual development.

- **University of Detroit Mercy** has a "Mission and Identity" office that engages staff and faculty from a variety of programs to help them assimilate and incorporate the university's mission and values into their work. These programs involve discussion and self-reflection about the participant's own spiritual development.

- **Virginia Wesleyan College** provides professional development support for faculty whose interests include research and teaching on spirituality.

Other practices:

- **Berea College** occasionally supports opportunities for professional development by covering travel to conferences, seminars, or workshops that enhance professional competence to support students' spiritual development.

- The Office of Spiritual Life at **California Baptist University** offers opportunities for staff and faculty to participate in spiritual activities together. Faculty are encouraged to share their stories of faith in the classroom.

- **Emmaus Bible College** has held professional development days related specifically to spiritual formation and the spiritual lives of American teenagers.

- **Fontbonne University** sends two faculty members a year to Collegium, a program in which members who work at Catholic institutions of higher education talk about how their work is a work of faith. Those who have attended over the years now organize a mini-Collegium meeting on campus once a year.

- Gordon College: The 2009 Fall Faculty Workshop was devoted to the theme of spiritual formation, as faculty discussed strategies for addressing spiritual development through the blending of curriculum and co-curriculum. The workshop focused especially on issues of teaching methods for spiritual development, and examined advising and mentoring outside of the classroom. Faculty also have prayer groups and hold semi-monthly Faculty Forums, which allow them to present their scholarly work, and often touch on issues of personal and spiritual development in their own lives and careers.

- Harding University provides funding to faculty members who lead "religious campaigns" during the summer.

- Presbyterian College discusses students' spiritual development in new faculty orientation.

- Rockhurst University has a number of opportunities for faculty and staff to engage in reflection. The campus offers lunch sessions that encourage reflection on some aspect of religious identity. The vice president for mission and ministry and director of human resources facilitate conversations in academic departments and administrative units about the mission and purpose of the university. The university offers overnight retreats for faculty and staff with focused reflection on the university's mission in light of their own values and purposes.

- Faculty conversations, presidential seminars, and new employee orientation at Sacred Heart University all address issues of spirituality.

- The question of faith integration at Southern Wesleyan University shows up in the new faculty orientation course called "Faculty Cornerstone." It is also a frequent topic of faculty development workshops.

- Staff members at Toccoa Falls College are allowed to take regular work time to meet with students in Barnabas Groups, which are the college's primary venue for helping students address life questions, cope with stress, and learn to care. These groups of six to 10 students are facilitated by faculty, staff, and upperclassmen. They meet weekly, and they focus on interaction, transformation, and life application.

- The Chaplain's Office at Trinity Christian College assists in the orientation of new staff and leads sections on the faith tradition and religious commitments of the college. Staff and faculty are required to submit faith statements in their application materials, which are updated at every re-appointment.

- At Union College, encouraging dialogue about students' spirituality is a topic integral to all faculty training. It is woven into both their training and dialogue, and demonstrated in their interactions with students.

Opportunities for Faculty and Staff to Explore Spirituality

Campuses can find creative ways to encourage faculty and administrators to explore their own spiritual journeys. Faculty and staff who are actively engaged in advancing their own spiritual development might have opportunities to share with colleagues lessons they have learned, or challenge faculty who are skeptical of such work. Senior colleagues who see the value of participating in efforts to support students' spiritual development can mentor and encourage junior colleagues to find ways to do so in their own work.

- Georgetown College has a Faculty Center that sponsors "vocation lunches" twice a semester, which allow faculty members to give a presentation on issues of spirituality, meaning, and purpose in their lives.

- Pepperdine University offers new faculty members a week-long faculty retreat to Italy or Argentina to discuss vocation, calling, and spiritual development. The university also provides a spiritual mentorship program that connects staff and faculty to students. Faculty and staff may also apply for paid leave for spiritual development.

- University of Denver has a program called "Soul and Role" which is designed to provide a safe space for faculty, staff, and administrators to reflect on the intersection between their inner lives and professional activities.

- University of Indianapolis houses a Faculty Development Center and an Ecumenical and Interfaith Programs Office that sponsors book discussions for faculty, staff, and administrators. Participants read a common resource, then discuss the content and application of the main ideas within campus contexts. The institution also offers discussion groups that enable campus personnel to reflect on their own spirituality, meaning, and purpose.

Other practices:

- **College of St. Benedict/St. John's University** has Lilly Foundation-sponsored programs that empower faculty, staff, and students to explore their spiritual journeys.

- **Lee University** offers a seminar every summer where faculty and staff explore the integration of faith and learning. At this retreat, faculty work on ways of engaging students in dialogues about faith and spiritual development.

- **Minot State University** started a spiritual wellness series for faculty and staff.

- At **Oakland City University**, faculty and staff are given time off for participating in spiritual development activities.

- At **Reinhardt University**, faculty and staff are nominated for **"This I Believe,"** a 30-minute talk on their deeply held beliefs.

- **Saint Louis University** has a chaplain for faculty and staff, and offers a wide array of programs designed to support them in their spiritual lives. These vary from short one- to three-hour programs to twilight retreats and weekend retreats. Faculty and staff also have the opportunity to participate in the Spiritual Exercises of St. Ignatius of Loyola in both their 30-day and nine-month formats.

RECOGNITION AND REWARDS

Campus leaders can communicate an institution's commitment to supporting students' spiritual development by recognizing students, staff, campus leaders, and faculty who exemplify spiritual qualities. Recognition can take various forms, ranging from awards presented at large-scale campus events such as convocations and commencements to highlighting the work of community members in campus magazines. For example:

- Bates College gives out the William Stringfellow Award to recognize students and other campus community members who work for peace and justice.

- LaGrange College offers the Inspiring the Soul Award for professors who inspire their students in the classroom.

- Mercyhurst College features an annual "Romero Award" and lecture for recipients who have made significant contributions to living their faith through justice.

- The University of the Incarnate Word annually honors one student and one faculty member, staff member or administrator with the CCVI Spirit Ward for exemplifying core values of the campus mission: faith, service, innovation, education, and truth. For each of the core values, an additional faculty member is recognized.

Many other institutions also support and recognize their outstanding community members for contributions to promoting spirituality (Alaska Pacific University, Andrews University, John Brown University, Oklahoma Baptist University, Troy University, University of St. Francis (Illinois), and West Virginia Wesleyan College).

DESIGNATED PHYSICAL SPACES

It is common for campuses to offer space to reflect, deliberate, or simply be quiet. Consideration of how the physical plant can foster spiritual development may convince campus leaders to dedicate some indoor or outdoor space for campus members to engage in ecumenical or interfaith worship, reflection, or meditation.

There are several ways to describe the spaces that campuses set aside. Many campuses today have meditation rooms or spaces. Others have prayer rooms, chapels, and sanctuaries. Some campuses with outdoor spaces have provided gardens, grottoes, labyrinths, prayer circles, and even simple sitting areas in less-trafficked parts of campus.

These spaces might vary in a number of dimensions. Campuses can determine where the indoor spaces will be housed: residence halls, student unions, campus centers. They can determine whether the décor and furniture are fixed or moveable, whether the space will be available at all hours, and whether it can be reserved. Campuses can also set guidelines for how the space may be used by individuals or by groups for meetings or religious services.

The many campuses that have designated physical spaces for reflection include:

- Albright College
- Bard College at Simon's Rock
- Barry University
- Belmont Abbey College
- Bethel College
- California Lutheran University
- Calvin College
- Campbellsville University
- College of New Rochelle
- Converse College
- Crossroads College
- Culver-Stockton College
- Curry College
- DePauw University
- Eastern Mennonite University
- Embry-Riddle Aeronautical University (Daytona Beach and Prescott)
- Emory & Henry College
- Endicott College
- Eureka College
- Florida State University
- Hiram College
- Hope International University
- Houghton College
- Howard Payne University
- Iowa State University
- Jewish Theological Seminary
- Kentucky Christian University
- Lancaster Bible College
- Limestone College
- Lycoming College
- Lynchburg College
- Lyon College
- Manchester College
- Manhattan College
- Martin Luther College
- Marymount Manhattan College
- Marywood University
- Menlo College
- Military College of South Carolina
- Misericordia University
- Moravian College and Moravian Theological Seminary
- Mount St. Mary's University
- Muhlenberg College
- Nebraska Christian College
- Oakwood University
- Oral Roberts University
- Our Lady of Holy Cross College
- Pace University in Pleasantville
- Philander Smith College
- Pontifical College Josephinum
- Portland State University
- Prairie View A&M University
- Ramapo College of New Jersey
- Rocky Mountain College
- Salve Regina University
- Southwestern Adventist University
- Southwestern College
- Spring Hill College
- St. Ambrose University
- St. John Fisher College
- St. Joseph Seminary College
- Stillman College
- Sweet Briar College
- Texas Lutheran University
- The Wesley Center at Ohio Northern University
- University of Dubuque
- University of Portland
- University of Saint Francis (Indiana)
- University of the Ozarks
- Vanguard University
- Wake Forest University
- Wheeling Jesuit University
- Winthrop University
- Wisconsin Lutheran College

FINANCIAL SUPPORT FOR INITIATIVES RELATING TO SPIRITUAL DEVELOPMENT

Campus leaders can facilitate students' spiritual development by establishing scholarships or fellowships to support individuals who show potential for living lives of charitable involvement or have exhibited behaviors that demonstrate an ethic of caring.

- Keuka College has a Spiritual Exploration Field Period Scholarship, which is available to students who can demonstrate that their field period will help them grow spiritually. The selection committee is composed of faculty, staff, and representatives from the alumni association. Students submit applications, complete an interview process and, if selected, make themselves available to talk about their field experiences with campus groups.

- University of California at Irvine has established a Dalai Lama Endowed Scholarship for students who have worked to advance compassion, peace, and ethics. In addition, an Ethics Fellow is chosen to help develop ethical guidelines for undergraduates, giving special attention to how students can develop tolerance of diverse lifestyles and values.

- Westfield State College Foundation (WSCF) recognizes and rewards the efforts of faculty, staff, and students who support students' spiritual development. Annual funding is provided by the WSCF to operate the Albert and Amelia Ferst Interfaith Center and compensate the staff. The WSCF also provides the Interfaith Programming Committee with an allocation to seek program proposals from the College community annually, and to award faculty, staff, and students with program grants for accepted program proposals.

- At Wesleyan College, the chaplain manages the Wesleyan Disciples program, a dozen or so students selected each year for scholarships, which require spiritual discipline and Bible study.

As we share these examples of promising practices from across the country, we also want to acknowledge the many practices that could not be included in this guidebook. We hope that the curricular, co-curricular, and campus-wide practices cited here will serve as examples for campuses to engage in similar practices and institutional efforts. In Part IV, we offer suggestions for considering how your institution might incorporate spirituality into your campus community.

PART IV
CONCLUDING THOUGHTS

PART IV:
CONCLUDING THOUGHTS

In developing this guidebook, our purpose was to present a selection of practices designed to facilitate students' spiritual development, which we gathered over the years. Reflecting upon the volume and variety of practices in which campuses are engaged, we arrived at a number of conclusions, two of which are worth noting here. First, interest and support for students' spiritual development are more widespread than we originally thought, and they are present at all types of campuses—religious and non-religious, public and private, research-oriented and liberal arts. This realization was both reassuring and encouraging to us, given our belief in attending to the education and development of the whole student.

Not surprisingly, we also observed that at campuses engaged in comprehensive practices, there was a clear sense of collaboration. At many of these campuses, multiple people from different campus units were involved in responding to our various invitations to share promising practices. Sometimes they submitted one response on behalf of many, other times they submitted multiple responses. This brings us full circle to a point we made earlier: initiatives are most successful and effective when campus units work in collaboration toward a common goal. Although supporting efforts to facilitate students' spiritual development may have a ripple effect on a campus' spiritual climate, the opposite may also be true. Efforts to make a campus' climate more amenable to spirituality may help the growth of nascent efforts to support students' spiritual development, and may also encourage the type of collaboration that is necessary for all effective initiatives.

In the previous sections, we provided background information on the *Spirituality in Higher Education* research project and longitudinal findings, presented a snapshot of spirituality on campus today, and shared samples of current promising practices. From here, we highlight briefly some institutional considerations that are important to take into account when considering approaches to incorporating spirituality into higher education. These include the impact of institutional culture, structure, and type, as well as considerations related to institutional mission and physical space. We conclude by sharing steps for creating a spiritual action plan to begin this work on your own campus.

INSTITUTIONAL CONSIDERATIONS

INSTITUTIONAL CULTURE, STRUCTURE, AND TYPE

Current efforts to move collectively toward integrating issues of meaning and purpose into higher education are often impeded. This is because existing campus cultures and structures do not encourage or support spiritual exploration or expression. Both explicit and implicit values shape the overall spiritual climate of an institution, which can also create and reinforce barriers to integrating spiritual dimensions into the campus culture. Resistance from administrators, faculty, staff, and even certain student populations can also inhibit this work. Through our research and interactions with various groups, we discovered that one of the largest barriers exists because of the uncertainty around what "spirituality" refers to and how it impacts a campus culture.

Institutional structure, including how departments and units collaborate and share resources, is another factor to consider when creating and instituting spiritual practices. Understanding how different offices can come together around a common goal to foster a healthy spiritual campus climate is a crucial step, making it possible to create strong practices that do not remain compartmentalized within selected institutional units.

Additionally, institutional type can either hinder or promote the integration of spirituality within the curricula and co-curricula on campuses. For example, conversations during the National Institute on Spirituality in Higher Education in 2006 and interviews with faculty in 2008-09 reflected a sense that at public institutions it tends to be much harder to agree whether colleges should be responsible for facilitating students' spiritual development. Narrowly defined conceptions of spirituality and concerns about maintaining the separation of church and state served as significant barriers to initiating and sustaining spirituality work. By comparison, it seemed more common to find established offices and individuals with clearly defined roles to support students' spiritual exploration at private institutions—even those that were nonsectarian—which signaled the institution's support for taking on this work.

INSTITUTIONAL MISSION

Mission and core values statements, or strategic plans are key documents to consider when establishing a foundation upon which to base efforts to promote spiritual development. Incorporation of words and phrases like *holistic, meaning and purpose, transformative,* and *student-centered* all suggest a connection to the larger work of integrating spirituality in higher education, providing implicit space and support for these ideas and associated practices.

Opportunities for administrators, faculty, staff, students, alumni, parents, and community members to reflect together on key institutional purposes, values, and practices are also important. Such programs and initiatives can facilitate creative thinking about how to most appropriately, and effectively, address spiritual considerations within specific campus communities. These dialogues can also encourage individual and collective investment in supporting students' spiritual development.

PHYSICAL SPACE

The physical environment and space on a campus impact students' ability to engage in spiritual exploration and dialogue and are also important factors in establishing a culture that is supportive of spiritual development work. Creating quiet and tranquil places indoors and outdoors, where individual reflection and contemplative practice naturally occurs, is one way to facilitate spiritual exploration on campus.

Additionally, for many students, spirituality is closely connected with their religious faith. Consequently, creating safe spaces where students of various faith traditions can freely practice is critical when promoting interfaith cooperation and religious pluralism on campus. While many campuses have churches, chapels, and other places of worship, these spaces are often tied to particular faith or belief systems. Non-denominational spaces—where students of widely different faiths or those who would simply like to learn more about certain faiths and religious traditions are actively welcomed—may also indicate an institution's support for students' spiritual development.

CREATING A SPIRITUALITY ACTION PLAN

Focusing on the five components below and considering the questions in Appendices B and C can lead to a "Spirituality Action Plan" to support spiritual development work on your campus.

1. Clarify your own thinking about spirituality: *Why is spirituality important to you within your role?*

2. Consider what possibilities or new initiatives exist in your department or field for integrating spirituality within your current responsibilities: *What is currently done and what gaps exist?*

3. Collaborate with other colleagues to brainstorm ideas and create action plans: *Who else is engaged and involved in this work on your campus?*

4. Connect with those who can help evaluate the feasibility of putting these ideas into action: *Who can help this work move forward?*

5. Create your own promising practices: *What practices might be most suitable for your campus?*

Overall, it takes an engaged and committed community of administrators, faculty, staff, and students to nurture the spiritual climate and culture within college and university campuses. The research, practices, and considerations shared in this guidebook highlight current efforts at hundreds of campus across the country, and we hope you find this information helpful for facilitating your own campus initiatives.

APPENDIX A:
SUMMER 2010 CAMPUS SURVEY

1. To your knowledge do any faculty at your institution:
    Response Categories: No, Not that I know of, Yes (one or two), Yes (more than two)

    - Offer courses designed to enhance knowledge and understanding of different religious/spiritual traditions?

    - Offer courses designed to encourage students to explore questions of meaning and purpose?

    - Employ contemplative practices (e.g. meditation, moments of silence) in the classroom?

    If you responded "yes" to any of the above, please briefly describe one or two examples.

2. Does your institution offer undergraduates opportunities to engage in the following co-curricular activities?
    Response Categories: No, Not that I know of, Yes

    - Events associated with a religious or spiritual awareness week

    - Interfaith dialogue

    - Religious life or interfaith council

    If you responded "yes" to any of the above, please briefly describe one or two examples.

3. Please estimate what percent of your students—
   (Enter number only)

   - Take at least one service learning course (an academic course)

   - Participate in study abroad

   - Participate in any form of community service/volunteer work

4. To your knowledge does your institution offer any other curricular or co-curricular programs that are designed to:
   Response Categories: No, Not that I know of, Yes

   - Promote a sense of caring or compassion for others?

   - Encourage students to explore life's "big questions"?

   - Promote a global worldview/global awareness or a greater appreciation of different races, cultures, religions, or nationalities?

   - Assist students in coping with stress or development?

   If you responded "yes" to any of the above, please describe.

5. Does your campus have any designated spaces dedicated to promoting meditation or quiet reflection?
   Response Categories: No, Yes
   (Please describe briefly.)

6. Does your institution encourage faculty, staff, or administrators to engage in dialogue about:
   Response Categories: No, Not that I know of, Yes

   - Ways to facilitate students' spiritual development?

   - Issues of spirituality, meaning, and purpose in their own lives?

   If you responded "yes" to either of the above, please briefly describe one or two examples.

7. Does your institution recognize and reward efforts by faculty, staff, and administrators who support students' spiritual development?
    Response Categories: No, Yes
    (Please describe briefly.)

8. Do you have any additional thoughts or comments?
    (Please describe briefly.)

9. May we contact you for follow-up information about your institution's programs?
    Response Categories: No, Yes
    If yes, please provide name, title, institution, phone number and e-mail address.

APPENDIX B:
CONSIDERATIONS FOR CAMPUS GROUPS

ADMINISTRATORS

Questions to Ask Yourself:
- How do the values of your institution's mission align with the spiritual qualities described in this guidebook?

- To what extent does your institutional culture support the idea of spiritual development?

- What existing campus relationships might help you encourage spiritual development on your campus?

- What is your institution currently doing to promote spiritual exploration on campus?

- What opportunities do you have within your institutional role/position to foster students' search for meaning and purpose?

Practices to Consider:
- Creating structure and support for other members of the campus to engage in promising practices

- Creating space for reflective practices

FACULTY

Questions to Ask Yourself:
- How does exploring spirituality, meaning, and purpose connect to undergraduate student development?

- What are your personal values and how do they intersect with your work as a faculty member?

Practices to Consider:

- Promoting interdisciplinary perspectives, critical thinking, problem solving, reflective judgment, synthesis of knowledge, and understanding of multiple perspectives

- Introducing reflective practices in the classroom

STUDENT AFFAIRS PROFESSIONALS

Questions to Ask Yourself:

- How does exploring spirituality, meaning, and purpose connect to undergraduate student development?

- What opportunities do you have to encourage students' spiritual development?

- What informal opportunities do you have to engage students in conversations about meaning and purpose?

Practices to Consider:

- Utilizing activities and programs that encourage students to question authority, and clarify values, knowledge, goals

- Employing self-reflection, journaling, meditation, and other reflective practices in your work with students

STUDENT LEADERS

Questions to Ask Yourself:

- How do your peers define spirituality?

- How important is it for you and your peers to develop spiritually?

- In your work with student clubs and organizations, where do you see opportunities to enhance spiritual development?

These questions can be downloaded as a handout at www.spirituality.ucla.edu.

APPENDIX C:
PERSONAL ACTION PLAN

After reading through the suggestions and practices in this guidebook, use the questions below to develop your own personal action plan to begin moving this work forward at your institution.

1. Do any of the ideas presented seem realistic to implement at your institution? Describe how you can modify or adapt them to meet your institution's needs.

2. Are there colleagues here or on your campus with whom you can collaborate to get this work started? Consider who you will need to connect with and when you can do this.

3. What obstacles, challenges, or barriers currently exist in your campus climate to prevent new initiatives from starting? Brainstorm strategies for overcoming these issues given your available resources.

4. What is a realistic time frame for implementation?
   ...next 6 months?
   ...next year?
   ...next five years?

5. What is one thing you can do today to get this work started?

This worksheet can be downloaded from our website at www.spirituality.ucla.edu.

References

Astin, A. W., Astin, H. S., & Lindholm, J. A. (2011). *Cultivating the spirit: How college can enhance students' inner lives*. San Francisco: Jossey-Bass.

Braskamp, L.A., Trautvetter, L. C., & Ward, K. (2006). *Putting students first: How colleges develop students purposefully*. Bolton, MA: Anker.

Publishing Chickering, A. W., Dalton, J. C., & Stamm, L. (2006). *Encouraging authenticity & spirituality in higher education*. San Francisco: Jossey-Bass.

Cohen, A. M. (1998). *The shaping of American higher education: Emergence and growth of the contemporary system*. San Francisco: Jossey-Bass.

Fowler, J. W. (1981). *Stages of faith: The psychology of human development and the quest for meaning*. San Francisco: Harper Collins.

Howe, N. & Strauss, W. (2007). *Millennials go to college: Strategies for a new generation on campus* (2nd Edition). Great Falls, VA: LifeCourse Associates.

Palmer, P. J. (1990). *The active life: A spirituality of work, creativity, and caring*. San Francisco: Jossey-Bass.

Parks, S. D. (2000). *Big questions, worthy dreams: Mentoring young adults in their search for meaning, purpose, and faith*. San Francisco: Jossey-Bass.

Reuben, J. A. (1996). *The making of the modern university: Intellectual transformation and the marginalization of morality*. Chicago and London: University of Chicago Press.

Trautvetter, L. C. (2007). Developing students' search for meaning and purpose. In G.L. Kramer and Associates (Eds.), *Fostering student success in the campus community* (pp. 236-261). San Francisco, CA: Jossey-Bass.

INDEX A:
KEY CONCEPTS

INDEX B:
PARTICIPATING INSTITUTIONS

CONTRIBUTORS

We wish to thank all those who submitted examples of the promising practices occurring at their campuses. Please note that some individuals may have left campuses since this guidebook went to print.

A

Alaska Pacific University, Douglas Lindsay
Albright College, Paul E. Clark
Allegheny College, Jane Ellen Nickell
Alma College, Carol Gregg
Alvernia University, Dr. Joseph J. Cicala
Alvernia University, Rev. Kevin Queally, TOR
American University, Joe Eldridge
Andrews University, Berrien Springs, MI., Frances Faehner
Andrews University, Berrien Springs, MI., Timothy P. Nixon
Antioch University New England, Katherine Clarke
Asbury University, Rev. Greg Haseloff
Ashland University, Dan Lawson
Atlanta Christian College, Samuel W. Huxford
Austin College, John Williams
Avila University, Dave Armstrong

B

Babson College, Denning Aaris
Bard College at Simon's Rock, Mary Marcy
Bard College, Bruce Chilton
Barry University, Rev. Scott O'Brien, OP
Barton College, George Solan
Bates College, Emily Wright-Timko
Bellarmine University, Melanie-Prejean Sullivan
Belmont Abbey College, Tricia Stevenson
Belmont University, Todd Lake

Beloit College, William Conover
Bentley University, Rev. Claude Grenache, A.A.
Berea College, Jeff B. Pool, Ph.D.
Berry College, Debbie Heida
Bethany College, Noni Strand
Bethel College, Dale R. Schrag
Bethel University, Edee Schulze
Biola University, Todd Pickett
Bloomsburg University of Pennsylvania, Maggie Gillespie
Boston College, Jennie Purnell
Brescia University, Pam Mueller
Bridgewater College, Robert R. Miller
Brooklyn College, Hershey H. Friedman
Bryn Athyn College, Ray Silverman
Bucknell University, Chris J. Boyatzis
Bucknell University, Rev. Thomasina A. Yuille
Butler University, Judith Cebula

C

Cabrini College, Christa Grzeskowiak
CalArts, Yvonne Guy
California Baptist University, John Montgomery
California Institute of Integral Studies, Mariana Caplan
California Institute of Integral Studies, Jorge N. Ferrer
California Lutheran University, Leanne Neilson
California Poly State University San Luis Obispo, Ken Barclay

California State University, San Bernardino,
    Luz Lara
Calvin College, Claudia Beversluis
Calvin College, Mary Hulst
Calvin College, Shirley J. Roels
Campbell University, Dr. Dennis N. Bazemore
Campbellsville University, Ed Pavy
Canisius College, Dr. Scott Chadwick
Canisius College, Sandra Estanek
Cardinal Stritch University, Jim Gannon, ofm
Carleton College,
    Carolyn Fure-Slocum & Bev Nagel
Carnegie Mellon University, Amy Burkert
Carnegie Mellon University, Indira Nair
Carroll College, Helena, MT,
    Dr. Jim Hardwick
Carroll College, Paula McNutt
Catawba College, Kenneth W. Clapp
Cedar Crest College, Carol Pulham
Cedarville University, Robert K. Rohm
Centenary College of New Jersey, Dave Jones
Center for Contemplative Mind in Society,
    Beth Wadham .
Centre College, Rick Axtell
Cheyney University of Pennsylvania,
    Etta G. Baldwin
Chowan University, Mari Wiles
Cincinnati Christian University, Jon Weatherly
Claremont Graduate University and California
    State Polytechnic University, Carol Bliss
Claremont Graduate University,
    Peter Drucker School of Management,
    Jeremy P. Hunter
Cleveland Hillel Foundation, Gary Coleman
Coastal Carolina University, Haven Hart
College of Mount Saint Vincent, Dianna Dale
College of Mount Saint Vincent,
    Cecilia Harriendorf, SC
College of Mount St. Joseph,
    Alan deCourcy & Andrea Stiles
College of New Rochelle, The, Dorothy Escribano

College of Notre Dame of Maryland,
    Melissa Lees
College of St. Benedict/St. John's University,
    Rita Knuesel
College of the Holy Cross, Paul F. Harman, S.J.
College of Saint Rose, The, Joan Horgan
College of Saint Rose, The,
    Rev. Christopher DeGiovine
Colorado College, Kate Holbrook
Conception Seminary College,
    Elizabeth McGrath
Concordia University Wisconsin, Steve Smith
Converse College, Jeffrey H. Barker
Corban University, Matt Lucas
Corban University, Nancy Hedberg
Cornell College (Iowa),
    Rev. Catherine Quehl-Engel
Cornerstone University, Gerald Longjohn, Jr.
Creighton University, Patrick J. Borchers
Crossroads College, Rick D. Walston
Culver-Stockton College, Brent Reynolds
Curry College, Terry Hofmann

D

Daemen College, Rev. Cassandra L. Salter-Smith
Dakota Wesleyan University,
    Rev. Brandon Vetter
Dallas Christian College, Mark C. Worley
Davidson College, Robert C. Spach
DePaul University, Mark Laboe
DePauw University, Rev. Kate Smanik
DeSales University, Fr. John Hanley, OSFS
Dillard University, Gail E. Bowman
Dominican University of California,
    Rev. Robert Haberman
Dominican University, Rosary College of Arts
    and Sciences, MaDonna Thelen

E

Earlham College, Kelly Burk
East Texas Baptist University, Alan Huesing

Eastern Connecticut State University, Rhona Free
Eastern Mennonite University,
   Brian Martin Burkholder
Eastern Mennonite University, Fred Kniss
Eastern Michigan University,
   Glenna Frank Miller
Eastern Oregon University, Camille Consolvo
Eastern University, Bettie Ann Brigham
Edgewood College, Mary Klink
Elmhurst College, Eileen G. Sullivan, Ph.D.
Elon University, Steven House
Embry-Riddle Aeronautical University,
   Daytona Beach, Richard H. Heist
Embry-Riddle Aeronautical University, Prescott,
   Jack Clevenger
Emmaus Bible College, Lisa Beatty
Emory & Henry College, Mary K. Briggs
Endicott College,
   The Rev. Dr. Stephen Butler Murray
Eureka College, Ken Baxter
Evangel University, John Plake
Evergreen State College, The, Art Costantino

F

Fairfield University, Ann Stehney
Fairfield University, Fairfield, CT,
   Michael J. Doody, SJ
Fairfield University, Ignatian Residential College,
   Elizabeth Dreyer
Fayetteville State University, Jon Young
Felician College, Sister Mary Rosita Brennan
Ferrum College, Wes Astin
Fisher College, Ann S. Clarke
Fisk University,
   Reverend Dr. Jason Richard Curry
Florida A&M University, Henry Kirby
Florida Southern College, Tim Wright
Florida State University, Mary Coburn
Fontbonne University, Sarah Boul
Franklin College, David Weatherspoon
Franklin Pierce University, Rev. Bill Beardslee

Franklin W. Olin College of Engineering,
   Rod Crafts
Furman University, Connie Carson
Furman University, John S. Beckford
Furman University, Linda Bartlett
Furman University, Vaughn Crowe-Tipton

G

Gallaudet University, Stephen F. Weiner
Gannon University, Deacon Stephen Washek
Gannon University, Ward McCracken
Geneva College, Keith Martel
Geneva College, Mike Loomis
George Fox University, Patrick Allen
George Mason University, Rose Pascarell
Georgetown College, Rosemary Allen
Georgia College and State University,
   Jennifer Graham
Gettysburg College, Christopher J. Zappe
Gettysburg College, Julie Ramsey
God's Bible School and College, Richard Miles
God's Bible School and College, Aaron Profitt
Gonzaga University, C. Hightower, S.J.
Gordon College, Mark Sargent
Goshen College, Bob Yoder
Grambling State University,
   Rev. Connie Breaux
Grand Valley State University,
   Aaron Klein Haight
Greensboro College, Robert Brewer
Grinnell College, Brad Bateman
Grove City College, Devi Wintrode
Guilford College, Adele Wayman

H

Hamline University, Nancy Victorin-Vangerud
Hampshire College, Liza M. Neal
Hannibal-LaGrange College, David J. Pelletier
Harding University, Bruce D. McLarty
Harding University, Larry R. Long
Hartwick College, Taralyn Loewenguth

Hastings College, David McCarthy
Haverford College, Jason McGraw
Hendrix College, Dr. Peg Falls-Corbitt
Heritage Christian University, Bill Bagents
Hiram College, Cheryl B. Torsney
Hope College, Richard Ray
Hope International University, J.J. Peterson
Houghton College, John Brittain
Howard Payne University, W. Mark Tew
Huston-Tillotson University, Donald Brewington

I

Illinois College of Optometry,
    Kelly A. Frantz
Immaculata University, Erin Ebersole
Indiana University-Purdue University Fort Wayne, George McClellan
Indiana Wesleyan University,
    Rev. Dr. Jim "Umfundisi" Lo
Institute of American Indian Arts,
    Dr. Ann Fielmyr
Iona College, Warren Rosenberg
Iowa State University, Arne Hallam
Iowa State University, Dan Black
Iowa State University, Jacinto F. Fabiosa
Iowa State University, Shari Reilly
Ithaca College, Michael Faber
Ithaca College, John Hochheimer

J

Jackson State University,
    Rev. Elbert McGowan
Jewish Theological Seminary,
    Stephen Garfinkel
John Brown University, Rod Reed
John Carroll University, John B Scarano
John Carroll University, Mark McCarthy
Johnson & Wales University, Charlotte,
    Tarun Malik
Johnson Bible College, Mark F. Pierce
Juniata College, David Witkovsky

K

Kansas State University, Matthew Cobb
Kentucky Christian University, Ronald W Arnett
Kenyon College, Rev. Karl Stevens
Kettering College of Medical Arts, Beverly Cobb
Kettering College of Medical Arts, Clive Wilson
Kettering College of Medical Arts,
    David VanDenburgh
Keuka College, Eric Detar
King College, Matt Peltier
King's College, Richard Hockman, C.S.C.

L

LaGrange College, Dr. Quincy Brown
Lancaster Bible College, Bob McMichael
Lawrence Technological University, Kevin Finn
Lawrence University, David Burrows
Lebanon Valley College,
    Rev. Paul M. Fullmer, Ph.D.
Lee University, Carolyn Dirksen
Lehigh University, Lloyd Steffen
Lesley University, Dr. Jared Kass
LeTourneau University, Harold Carl
Limestone College, Ron Singleton
Lincoln Memorial University, Dr. Ray Penn
Louisiana Tech University, Dr. Barry J. Morales
Loyola College Maryland, John Dennis, S.J.
Loyola Marymount University,
    Elena M. Bove, Ed. D.
Loyola University of Chicago,
    Jennifer G. Haworth
Lubbock Christian University, Randal Dement
Lycoming College,
    Sr. Catherine Ann Gilvary, IHM
Lynchburg College, Stephanie McLemore
Lyon College, Nancy McSpadden

M

Maharishi University of Management,
    Evan Finkelstein

Malone University, Will Friesen
Manchester College, Glenn Sharfman
Manhattan College, Lois Harr
Maranatha Baptist Bible College, Brian Trainer
Marquette University, Susan Mountin
Martin Luther College, Jeffrey Schone
Martin Methodist College, Rev. Laura Kirkpatrick
Marymount Manhattan College,
    Carol L. Jackson
Maryville College, Anne D. McKee
Maryville College, Jeff Fager
Maryville University, Stephen DiSalvo
Marywood University, Dr. Ray Heath
Marywood University,
    Sr Catherine Luxner, IHM
Massachusetts Institute of Technology,
    Robert M. Randolph
McNeese State University, Toby Osburn, Ed.D.
Menlo College, Yasmin Lambie-Simpson
Mercer University, Craig McMahan
Mercyhurst College, Gerard Tobin, PhD
Messiah College, Eldon Fry
Miami University, Richard Nault
Mid Atlantic Christian University, Nicole Jones
Mid Atlantic Christian University, Chris Stanley
MidAmerica Nazarene University,
    Randy Beckum
MidAmerica Nazarene University, Steve Ragan
Middlebury College, Laurel Jordan
Miles College, Dollie Howell Pankey
Military College of South Carolina, Tara McNealy
Mills College, Dr. Angela Batista
Minot State University, Kari Williamson
Misericordia University, Christine Somers
Misericordia University, Mary Hinton
Mississippi College, Eric Pratt
Mississippi State University, J. Scott Young
Missouri Southern State University,
    Darren Fullerton
Molloy College, Scott Salvato
Monmouth College, Jane Jakoubek

Monmouth College, Rev. Dr. B. Kathleen Fannin
Montclair State University, Esmilda Abreu
Montreat College, Becky Frawley
Moody Bible Institute, Tim Arens
Moravian College and Moravian Theological
    Seminary, Hopeton Clennon
Mount Aloysius College, Brad Hastings
Mount Mary College, Pam Schoessling
Mount St. Mary's University, David Rehm
Muhlenberg College, Peter Bredlau

N

Naropa University, Sherry Ellms
Nazareth College, Sara Varhus
Nebraska Christian College, David Huskey
Nebraska Methodist College, Daniel Johnston
Nebraska Wesleyan University, Mara Bailey
Neumann University, Melissa Hickey
Neumann University,
    Sr. Marguerite O'Beirne, OSF
North Greenville University, Dr. Steve Crouse
North Park University, Rich Johnson
Notre Dame College, Anthony Camino
Notre Dame College, Carol Ziegler, SND
Nyack College, Wanda Walborn

O

Oakland City University, Dr. James Pratt
Oakwood University, Rupert Bushner, Jr
Oberlin College and Conservatory of Music,
    Rev. Greg McGonigle
Occidental College, Rev. Susan E. Young
Ohio Dominican University, Fr. John J. Boll, O.P.
Ohio Northern University, Vernon F. LaSala
Oklahoma Baptist University, M. Dale Griffin
Oklahoma City University, Richard Hall
Olivet Nazarene University, Gregg Chenoweth
Olivet Nazarene University, Mark Holcomb
Oral Roberts University, Dr. Clarence V. Boyd, Jr.
Oregon Institute of Technology, Erin Foley
Ouachita Baptist University, Stan Poole

Our Lady of Holy Cross College, Mary Pat Barth
Our Lady of the Lake University,
    Gloria Urrabazo

P

Pace University in New York,
    Lisa Bardill Moscaritolo
Pace University in New York, Marijo O'Grady
Pacific Lutheran University, Eva Johnson
Paine College, Curtis Martin
Paine College, Dr. Luther B. Felder
Palm Beach Atlantic University, Bernie A. Cueto
Palm Beach Atlantic University, Mark Kaprive
Peace College, Ashley Griffith
Pennsylvania State University-Mont Alto, The,
    Kimberly Hoover
Pennsylvania State University–Schuylkill, The
    Donald C. Lindenmuth
Pepperdine University, Christopher Collins
Pfeiffer University, Doug Hume
Philander Smith College, Juliana Mosley
Piedmont College, Ashley Cleere
Pontifical College Josephinum, Dr. Michael Ross
Portland State University, Jackie Balzer
Prairie View A&M University,
    Charles H. Lewter, IV
Presbyterian College, Anita Gustafson
Presbyterian College, Bill McDonald
Prescott College, Laurie Silver
Princeton Theological Seminary, Ellen Charry
Providence College, Fr. Joseph J. Guido, O.P.
Purchase College State University of New York,
    Regina Abdou

Q

Queens University of Charlotte, J. Diane Mowrey
Queens University of Charlotte, Norris Frederick

R

Ramapo College of New Jersey, Patrick P. Chang
Regent University, Alfred P. Rovai

Regis University, Steve Jacobs
Regis University, Peter Rogers
Reinhardt University, Leigh Martin
Rhodes College, Michael R. Drompp
Rivier College, Mary Jane Silvia
Roberts Wesleyan College, Rev. Jonathan Bratt
Rochester College, Adam Hill
Rochester College, Brian Cole
Rockhurst University, Rev. Kevin Cullen
Rockhurst University, William Haefele
Rocky Mountain College, Rev Kristi Foster
Rollins College, Patrick J Powers
Roosevelt University, Eric Tammes
Rosemont College, Elizabeth Small
Rowan University, James O. Anderson

S

Sacred Heart University, Rev. Gerald Ryle
Saint Joseph's University, Thomas Sheibley
Saint Louis University, Fr. Joe Fortier, S.J.
Saint Louis University, Lisa Reiter
Saint Peter's College, Mary Sue Callan-Farley
Saint Peter's College, Michael L. Braden, S.J.
Saint Xavier University, Esther Sanborn
Salem College, Rev. Dr. Amy Rio-Anderson
Salve Regina University, Dean de la Motte
Salve Regina University, John Rok
Sam Houston State University, David Payne
Sam Houston State University, John Yarabeck
Santa Clara University, Diane Jonte-Pace
Santa Clara University, Thomas Plante
Santa Clara University, Valerie Sarma
Santa Clara University, Jack Treacy, SJ
Santa Clara University,
    Br. Keith Douglass Warner
Savannah State University, Dr. Mary C. Wyatt
Schreiner University, Rev. Gini Norris-Lane
Seattle Universitiy, Mike Bayard, SJ
Seton Hall University, Greg Burton
Sewanee: The University of the South,
    Eric Hartman

Shepherd University, Sharon Kipetz
Silver Lake College of the Holy Family,
    Deacon Paul Gleichner
Simpson College, Angela Gafford
Skidmore College, Muriel Poston
Smith College, Frédérique Apffel-Marglin
Smith College, Jennifer L Walters
Southern Adventist University, Robert Young
Southern Arkansas University, Donna Y. Allen
Southern Illinois University Carbondale,
    Larry Dietz
Southern Oregon University, Jonathan Eldridge
Southern Vermont College, Al DeCiccio
Southern Wesleyan University, Keith Iddings
Southwestern Adventist University, Bill Kilgore
Southwestern Christian University,
    Dr. Reggies Wenyika
Southwestern College, Rev. Ashlee Alley
Spelman College, Beletia Marvray Diamond
    and Frank T. Martin
Spelman College, Lisa Rhodes
Spring Hill College, George Sims
Springfield College, David Braverman
Springfield College, Springfield, MA,
    David L. C. McMahon
St. Ambrose University, Rev. Charles Adam
St. Bonaventure University, Robert M. Donius
St. John Fisher College, Rick DeJesus-Rueff
St. John's University (Minnesota),
    Doug Mullin, OSB
St. John's University, Pamela Shea-Byrnes
St. Joseph Seminary College, Jude Lupinetti
Stanford University, Ronald Barrett
Stanford University, William (Scotty) McLennan
Stanford University, Abigail Nathanson
Stanford University,
    Rabbi Patricia Karlin-Neumann
Stanford University, Joanne Sanders
Stetson University, Michael Fronk
Stillman College, Dr. Sharon E. Whittaker
SUNY Geneseo, Carol S. Long

SUNY Maritime College,
    The Rev. John T. Farrell, Ph.D.
SUNY Potsdam, Christine Strong
SUNY Potsdam, Harvey A. Smith
SUNY Potsdam, Margaret Madden
Susquehanna University, Mark Radecke
Sweet Briar College, Jonathan D. Green

T

Taylor University, Skip Trudeau
Tennessee Tech University, Marc L. Burnett
Texas Christian University,
    Rev. Angela Kaufman
Texas Lutheran University, Greg Ronning
Toccoa Falls College, Jeff Gangel
Trevecca Nazarene University, Brent Tallman
Trinity Christian College, Willis Van Groningen
Trinity College, Allison Read
Trinity Lutheran College, Jeffrey Mallinson
Troy University, Barbara Patterson
Tufts University, David O'Leary

U

Union College (Nebraska), Rich Carlson
Universidad del Este- Puerto Rico,
    Carmen Socomo Rodriguez Mercado
University of Arizona, Jenny Lee
University of California, Berkeley,
    Michael Nagler and Doug Oman
University of California, Irvine,
    Manuel Gomez
University of California, Irvine, Nancy Minear
University of California, Los Angeles, Pam Viele
University of California, San Diego,
    Gary Anderson
University of California, San Diego,
    Barbara Sawrey
University of California, Santa Barbara,
    Katya Armistead
University of California, Santa Cruz,
    Alma Sifuentes

University of Dayton, Crystal Caruana Sullivan
University of Denver, Gary Brower
University of Detroit Mercy, Gary Wright, SJ
University of Dubuque, Rev. Jim Gunn
University of Great Falls, Richard L. McDowell
University of Houston-Downtown,
 Tommy Thomason
University of Indianapolis,
 Rev. Dr. L. Lang Brownlee
University of Iowa, Beth Ingram
University of Kentucky, Betsy Mahoney
University of Louisiana (Lafayette),
 Jeff Sandoz
University of Mary Hardin-Baylor,
 James Cohagan
University of Massachusetts Amherst,
 Mary Anne Bright
University of Massachusetts Lowell,
 Charlotte Mandell
University of Michigan, Malinda Matney
University of Missouri, Cathy Scroggs
University of New Hampshire,
 The Waysmeet Center @ UNH, Rev. Larry
 Brickner-Wood
University of North Texas, Paul F. Goebel
University of Oklahoma – Norman Campus,
 Nancy L. Mergler
University of Pittsburgh, Shawn E. Brooks
University of Portland,
 Br. Donald J. Stabrowski, C.S.C., Ph.D.
University of Redlands, Fran Grace
University of Rhode Island, Tom Dougan
University of Richmond, Craig Kocher
University of Saint Francis (Indiana),
 Janet Patterson
University of San Diego, Michael Lovette-Colyer
University of San Diego, Mark Peters
University of San Francisco, The,
 Donal Godfrey
University of Southern California, Varun Soni
University of Southern Maine, Betty Robinson

University of St. Francis (Illinois),
 Sharon Frederick, OSF
University of St. Thomas, Don Beyers
University of St. Thomas, Erich Rutten
University of St. Thomas, John Malone
University of Tampa, Stephanie Russell Holz
University of the Incarnate Word, Beth Villarreal
University of the Incarnate Word,
 Sister Walter Maher
University of the Ozarks, Daniel Taddie
University of the Pacific,
 Rev. Dr. Donna McNiel
*University of Toronto, Ontario Institute for
 Studies in Education,* Jack Miller
University of Turin, Italy, Enzo Giorgino
University of Virginia, Julie Caruccio
University of Wisconsin-Eau Claire,
 Marc Goulet
Utica College, Annette L. Becker

V

Vanderbilt University, John Tarpley
Vanguard University, Vince Beresford
Vassar College, Samuel Speers
Vaughn College, Sharon DeVivo
Villanova University, Kail C. Ellis
Virginia Commonwealth University,
 Linda Hancock
Virginia Wesleyan College, Timothy G. O'Rourke

W

Wake Forest Divinity School, Katherine Amos,
 Samuel F. Weber, & Sam Stevenson
Wake Forest University, Timothy L. Auman
Walla Walla University,
 Ginger Ketting-Weller
Warner University, Michael Sanders
Warner University, William M. Rigel
Wartburg College, Ramona S. Bouzard
Webster University, Anastasia (Stacy) Henning
Wesleyan College, Vivia Fowler

West Texas A&M University, James Hallmark
West Virginia Wesleyan College,
    Angela Gay Kinkead
West Virginia Wesleyan College, Larry R. Parson
Western Connecticut State University,
    Dr. Walter B. Bernstein
Westfield State College, Mr. Daryl Hendery
Westmont College, Dr. Bill Wright
Wheeling Jesuit University,
    Christine Ohl-Gigliotti
Wheeling Jesuit University, James Brogan
Whittier College, Joy Hoffman
Wilberforce University, Richard Allen Williams
Wiley College, Ernest J. Plaata
Wiley College, Joseph L. Morale
Willamette University, Charles Wallace`
William Jessup University, Kay Llovio
William Jewell College, Andrew Pratt
William Woods University, Travis Tamerius
Wilson College, Rev. Rosie Magee
Winthrop University, Frank Ardaiolo
Wisconsin Lutheran College, Nathan J. Strobel
Wittenberg University,
    Rev. Rachel Sandum Tune

X

Xavier University of Louisiana,
    Loren Blanchard

Y

Yale University, Sharon Kugler
York College of Pennsylvania, Louise Worley

Made in the USA
Lexington, KY
21 July 2011